How to *Really* Manage Inventories

How to *Really* Manage Inventories

Hal Mather

McGraw-Hill Book Company

New York St. Louis San Francisco Auckland Bogotá Hamburg
Johannesburg London Madrid Mexico Montreal New Delhi
Panama París São Paulo Singapore Sydney Tokyo Toronto

Library of Congress Cataloging in Publication Data

Mather, Hal.
  How to really manage inventories.

  Includes index.
  1. Inventory control. I. Title.
HD40.M37 1984   658.7'87   83-25554
ISBN 0-07-040892-0

1234567890   BKP/BKP   8987654

ISBN 0-07-040892-0

The editors for this book were William A. Sabin and Sheila H.
Gillams, the designer was Dennis Sharkey, and the production
supervisor was Sally Fliess. It was set in Palatino by Monotype
Composition Co., Inc.
Printed and bound by The Book Press.

To my wife, Jean, for her long-suffering patience, willingness to retype this manuscript several times, and acceptance of vacations spent behind a typewriter.

Contents

Chapter 5   Disturbed Flow Rates   70

Chapter 6   Inventory as a Dampener   93

Chapter 7   Input-Output Control   113

Chapter 8   Right Inventory Level   138

Chapter 9   Role of Systems   153

Preface

A better title for this book might have been "All Inventory Management Is Exactly Wrong." Whether this would have created the same amount of interest as the current title is questionable. But my thesis is that all inventory management is exactly wrong, and this will be the thrust of the book.

Scientific inventory management is a key contributor to business problems and our boom-and-bust cycles. Extracts of articles from a number of sources will be used in Chapter 11 to prove this statement. Dated materials are used at the risk of outdating this book quickly. But that is my objective. If I can get inventory management changed for the better, thus stopping its negative influences, I will have achieved my objective. However, history has a remarkable tendency to repeat itself. If you are reading this book several years after its publication, my guess is that simply moving the dates on these reprints forward by a few years will make them seem very current.

The tough job is to persuade you to try an alternative approach to scientific inventory management. A new method is not difficult in a technical sense. The management of inventories and their side effects, order flow rates, is ridiculously easy. Studying a bathtub will show you how to manage them. Getting a new approach accepted by you, a member of a management team or an inventory practitioner, is the tough part. You tend to retreat into sophisticated mathematics where inventory management is concerned, with big, expensive computer systems to massage the data. But these will never manage inventories no matter what the college professors, hardware vendors, and software houses tell you.

An even tougher job is to suggest how to combat inventory's evil influence on our economic cycles. I am not sure this is possible or even desirable. So I have restricted my comments mainly to how factory owners, distributors, or retailers can insulate themselves from the worst external effects while keeping tight control on their own businesses. I'll leave the total economy to someone more qualified to solve the bigger picture.

I *will* relate the effects of inventory decisions made throughout the economy on order flow rates and the boom-and-bust cycle. This is done with some trepidation as I am not an economist, at least no more than an armchair one. I hope the economists of the world forgive this intrusion by a neophyte into their field, but intrude I must. Inventories and their management are just not understood by most of the economic fraternity, which includes economists, business writers, and economics professors. Even managers of businesses that use inventories, for example, manufacturers, distributors, and retailers, are confused and confounded by inventories. Stock levels seem to have a will of their own. Like an unruly child, inventories are never where you want them, when you want them.

Inventories and order flow rates are an integral part of the economy of every country. Read any article or book on economics and you will find that it refers to the performance of inventories and order flow rates. The key point missing from these writings is why inventories and order flow rates behave as they do. Oh yes, economics books discuss inventories in a macro manner, but inventories are not created by macro decisions. Millions of individual decisions made by thousands of people about specific parts or raw materials create inventories. It's very much a micro management process not a macro one. It's a little like the old saw about decisions made by a husband and wife. He makes the "big" decisions, such as whom to vote for in the next election, and she makes the "small" ones, such as when to buy a car. Top-level managers set company policy, but low-level people spend the company's assets.

Why inventories behave as they do will be my major emphasis. This will not be done through macro analysis but by explaining the current state-of-the-art systems and techniques used for inventory management. I can safely say that from an economic point of view, and in most cases from an individual business point of view, most current inventory theories, systems, and management techniques *are* exactly wrong. Not only are they wrong, but they are damaging our economy and businesses by scientifically amplifying small changes in real end-consumer demand into the boom-and-bust cycles we experience regularly.

Case Study—Manufacturing in America

Inventory management and its effect on business and the economy is too broad a subject to tackle at one time, so I will reduce the scope of the discussion. After all, inventory management is a micro decision process. I would like to focus your attention on manufacturing companies in America. I have chosen manufacturing because, from an inventory management perspective, manufacturing is more complex than distribution or retailing. I hope this does not alienate the distributors and retailers reading this book. The parallels to your particular situation should be clear and should prove that you are also the culprits and victims of poor inventory performance. Where your problems differ significantly from those of manufacturers, I have explained these differences in detail.

I have reduced the scope to just America in order to prove—by using the articles from various American trade journals and newspapers—that the view of reality I present is really happening. But the same actions and effects that occur in America also occur elsewhere, as can be seen by reading trade journals and newspapers from other countries.

About This Book

Following are the key topics covered in this book.

Inventory Management   Inventory management is very much a micro decision process, and as such is very much out of control. There are too many individual decisions being made to suggest that any control exists. The sum of these many decisions never adds up to the totals desired. This is obviously true when few if any managers are willing to state they have the "right" level of inventory for their business and that it has been "right" consistently for a number of years.

Lead Times   Lead times influence economic statistics and business psychology out of all proportion to their real value. Lead-time changes affect the flow rates of orders between supplier and user, in most cases with no relation to real demand. But economists regularly report how order flow rates relate to industry shipments. If orders are above shipments, the economy is booming; if below, we're in a recession. Businesspeople look at backlogs of orders as a measure of their company's health. Big backlogs mean their company is healthy. Low backlogs mean their company is in trouble. Both these ideas will be debunked and shown to be ridiculous.

Emotion   According to the textbooks, inventory management is a scientific subject. Nothing could be more wrong. Emotion at all levels in a company really manages inventories, half the time resulting in too much inventory, the other half in too little. Getting control of emotion is the most difficult job for a management team.

Multitiered System   The production and distribution system in a country is multitiered. Many producers and distributors are linked together, with goods passing eventually from raw-material producers to the end consumers. Any one company within this chain is affected by decisions made by downstream companies, and they in turn affect upstream companies with their decisions. The most damaging decisions to all parties are those made regarding inventories. But as stated earlier, inventory decisions are not under control. So we are simultaneously the culprits and victims of these out-of-control decisions.

Systems   Today's state-of-the-art inventory replenishment systems are exactly wrong. Yes, you heard me: exactly wrong.

These systems do not have inventory management as their goal. They are item managers. Inventory systems manipulate detailed mathematical relations and try to make many right decisions on many separate items. The assumption is that if all these decisions are made correctly, on all these details, then the total will be correct. Baloney! That's about as valid as selling seats on an airplane without knowing how big the airplane is—just hoping it's the right size. But it will always be either too big or too small, just like inventories. This means a major restructuring of inventory systems is necessary if we ever hope to manage inventories correctly.

Measurements The traditional performance measuring system in a business is financially oriented. But as much as the financial people of the world say they are interested in reducing inventories, there are no clear suggestions in their systems of how to reduce them, or even of how much inventory is needed to run a business to maximize return on investment. Even more devastating is the fact that many of their measures are designed to increase inventories, but not one is designed to reduce them. Just look at the profit and loss statement and balance sheet of your company and show me where the pressure on inventories is. There's not even a line showing how much they cost other than the interest payment line. But interest payments may be due to factors other than financing inventories. And what about the lost opportunity cost of tying up capital in inventory rather than in productive assets or other good investments? Where does that show up? Answer: It doesn't. So other measures are needed if we really want to manage ourselves out of this mess. And we'd better find out just how much inventory is needed to run the business to maximize return on investment.

Top Down, Not Bottom Up Mr. or Ms. General Manager, you are delegating too much control to too low a level. Inventories are too important to be left to the specialists. You have to take charge and decide how much inventory you can afford. Then you'd better put the controls in place to ensure this is all you get, no more and no less. Use any other approach and sophisticated mathematics will slowly drive you bankrupt. Get control now before it's too late, for the benefit of your company and our economy.

Economic Disruption Anyone who has been in business more than just a few years knows about the business cycle. It's a fact of life, repeating almost exactly every 4 years. Check the statistics if you don't believe me. One of the real contributors to this cycle is mismanaged inventories. All economists talk about inventories and suggest they amplify the boom-and-bust cycle but don't explain why. Some even look to inventory growth to pull us out of recessions; why can't they see inventory growth as the seed of the *next* recession? Inventories are just like other natural phenomena: what goes up must come down. So if inventories can pull us out of recession by going up, they can plunge us deeper into recession by going down. Why can't they be stabilized? Why can't they operate against the cycle, growing when business drops off and dropping when business picks up? That way they would become a real dampener on the business cycle instead of an amplifier. But to do this means getting them under control. And under control they're not.

You'll find these statements, as well as many others, clearly defined in the chapters to come. More importantly you should come away with a much clearer idea of how to combat the negative influences of inventory management. If you apply these concepts, your business will be that much better for it and our economy will stop its vicious oscillation to the benefit of all.

A Retrospective

Some of the ideas expressed in this book, coming as they do from someone who has consulted and lectured on inventory management for 10 years, may sound a little strange. But I have never shrunk from controversy when the accepted view has been proved wrong. I'll let you decide if it's wrong or not after reading the evidence I present.

The key point is I did not start out with these feelings. I was a practitioner for many years in production and inventory control, worked on manufacturing systems for scheduling and inventory management, and ended up as a materials manager. I learned enough about the current theory of inventory management to become certified as a fellow by the American Production and Inventory Control Society. In the early days of my consulting and lecturing I followed the standard line. But as I watched company after company fail to manage inventories well, no matter what systems were implemented, doubts started to grow. The economic consequences of poor inventory management were simply the final evidence that caused this book to be written.

I have used a conversational style including some humor throughout. This is a departure from normal business books on this subject but I know how dry this subject can be. I hope this does not detract from my message and that it doesn't give the impression I'm not serious. Nothing could be further from the truth; I'm deadly serious. My only reason for using this style is to help you, the reader, finish the book and achieve the improvements its suggestions can make.

Hal Mather

About the Author

Hal Mather is president of Hal Mather, Inc., Atlanta, Georgia. He has held a variety of positions in industry and is now a world-renowned consultant to top-level managers. He has had articles published in the *Harvard Business Review* and several other professional magazines, and he is the technical editor of *Inventories & Production* magazine.

Chapter One

Confusion in the Ranks

The majority of top-level managers, especially after a couple of stiff drinks, will admit they are not in control of their businesses. The business operates as if it had a mind of its own. Sure, there are exceptions, top managers who really do control their businesses. If you are one of those or working for one, then what I have to say will be of limited value to you, other than to see how others operate. Or maybe you think you are in control but are not. You could be my best candidate for critical self-evaluation and, it is hoped, constructive change.

Most top managers are not steering the ship; they're along for the ride. Their objectives always seem to be something they are passing through, especially inventory objectives. The right level is either what they had in the past or what they will have fleetingly in the future.

Surprises are common. Suddenly sales are 30 percent over forecast and everyone celebrates. But why are sales up? What caused it? The sales manager is quick to take credit. It's because of his or her efforts, the advertising campaign that finally paid off, or the catchall "We are gaining market share." The chief engineer also takes credit: "It's because of the superior design." Manufacturing people claim it's the high-quality products or good customer service. But no one knows for sure. And in most cases it's not internal influences that made the sales go up, but external ones. But who is willing to admit that external influence is the key?

When sales drop precipitously, the reverse occurs. It's never the fault of people inside the plant. "The economy is in recession" is heard as the reason or, "It's foreign competition dumping products in our markets." But it's neither of these reasons. Other external influences are causing most of these changes.

Economists and business forecasters are just as confused. When one of them predicts the gross national product (GNP) for a quarter and the actuals come in close, that person is considered to have a better forecasting model. But if that were true, he or she should consistently forecast GNP levels accurately. No one business forecaster has that track record. Luck more than science seems the key.

The forecasting of interest rates is just as unpredictable as the GNP. Even forecasts for a couple of months in the future are wildly off. Doesn't this prove other factors are at work that have not been considered?

Some of the tenets of economic thinking are dead wrong. The statement "When the flow of orders for products is higher than the shipments of the same products, the economy is healthy" is one such incorrect belief. But many general managers happily operate their businesses with orders booking faster than shipments, thus creating large, "healthy" backlogs. But "large, healthy backlogs" is a contradiction in terms. And the statement about order flows will later be proved wrong and shown to be false demand, the worst kind because of its cyclical nature. It's those millions of inventory decisions, not real demand, that trigger order flows. When order flows are higher than shipments, it means that sometime in the future, order flows will drop below shipments to compensate. And then we will tell ourselves we are in a recession and things are bad. But in neither case have order flows represented the real state of end-consumer demand. Shipments, although not an accurate predictor of demand, are a much closer predictor than order flows. But we look at order flows and so make statements about demand, boom times, and recession that are untrue.

A business can no longer afford to be wrong; the costs of errors are just too high. Competition is significantly keener today than only a few years ago. The reductions in tariff barriers negotiated in the 1960s now allow goods to easily move across national boundaries. So our competition is not only domestic companies but companies in other countries with a completely different set of expectations, different costs, and a different environment from ours. Our success or failure to compete with overseas products has huge implications for our standard of living, balance of payments, employment opportunities, and our total economy.

The recent increase in the cost of money is making debt an onerous burden. With interest rates in the mid-1950s at 4 and 5 percent, asset management was of little concern. In the 1960s interest rates edged up to 6 and 7 percent. The 1970s saw growth to 12 and 14 percent. The 1980s have set the record so far with interest rates topping 20 percent. Excess or unproductive assets in this climate cannot be tolerated. Yet most manufacturers have huge excess and unproductive assets. They are called inventories on the balance sheet and show up as "current" assets, which they are not. They are largely liabilities. In too many cases you have what nobody wants and do not have what customers are buying. Do you need any more proof you are not in control? How could this happen if you were? I think it was Charles Revson of Revlon who said, "All management errors end up as inventories. They are the monuments to our failure to manage."

The cost of financing inventories has to be paid in the prices we charge for products. Even if we are cash rich, putting money into inventory instead of a fast payback investment is a cost the product price must support. If we could manage inventories better, our prices could be lower and more competitive.

A worse problem is the freezing of limited assets—money—in nonproductive uses—inventory. Companies need cash to fund research and development in order to produce new products; cash to finance newer, more productive machines; cash to develop new markets; and cash to grow in other ways. If too much cash is frozen in inventory, either some of these opportunities must be bypassed or borrowing must provide the necessary funds. But at today's interest rates, borrowings become a tremendous drain on a company's profits, inhibiting real cash generation even further. The improved management of inventories can free large reserves of money quickly, an action crucial to business health and the health of our economy.

Logistics Systems

Much effort has been spent in the last 20 years on inventory planning and scheduling. Powerful business computers provided the resource capable of performing the huge numbers of calculations needed to simulate a factory or manage a distributor's inventory. The American Production and Inventory Control Society (APICS) was formed in 1957 and became the fastest growing professional society in the United States with branches and affiliates around the world. Many consultants, data processing people, practitioners, and a few college professors helped define the body of knowledge in the field of inventory control. Examinations are routinely held on inventory management and its related disciplines. But successful companies are rare if success is measured by low inventories, high customer service, and a productive work force. And even worse, some companies that achieved these goals did so fleetingly. They quickly deteriorated back to the norm of mediocrity. The logistics system was not changed, so *it* was not the key to success or failure.

Systems and computers are assumed to have logical relations and logical outputs and most do. Take airline reservation systems, for example. They overbook on the basis of past experience of no-shows. But logistics systems provide illogical outputs, subject to emotional overrides along the way by planners, schedulers, buyers, and supervisors. Using seemingly logical but actually illogical, emotion-laden information guarantees failure. At this point I have probably alienated all the practitioners, computer hardware and software people, consultants, and educators who make a living from logistics systems. But face the facts. Show me the successes and failures.

You and I know we have far fewer of the former than the latter. And bigger computers equipped with more sophisticated systems that process information faster are not the solution. The solution lies in understanding what is wrong with the control systems. Sad to say, most of our logistics systems do not even come close to control systems.

The terms I will use to describe logistics systems are familiar to anyone involved with inventory management. The two techniques that trigger replenishment actions in a factory or distribution network, "order-point planning" and "material requirements planning," are well known and their differences clear. I will touch on these in Chapter 4. I will also show that although these terms and techniques are familiar to most, they are understood by few. Even more important, they are illogical and riddled with emotion. This is damaging our companies and the total economy. The result is that we invite competitors into our markets, many from overseas, and they rarely leave. We go crying to the government about unfair competition and the need for tariff protection when it was our failure to manage in the first place that gave the competition the opening.

It should be clear that order-point planning and material requirements planning are the triggering mechanisms that commit company assets. You can talk about long-range business strategies, new markets, new products, and promotional campaigns all you like, but the execution of these plans is a function of the logistics techniques. Here is one source of surprises. Many top-level managers think when they make high-level business decisions that execution of these wishes is automatic. Nothing could be further from the truth. Many systems, techniques, numbers, and, above all, people are inserted between high-level plans and actual execution. Frequently, these plans are changed during the translation process with no feedback loop telling top-level managers that the plans are changed and by how much.

Reflect upon your last long-range business planning meeting if you don't believe me. Didn't you spend a fair amount of time discussing the prior meeting's decisions and how few were actually executed? How confident are you that this year's decisions will be executed? Do you know how overall aggregate decisions made by top-level managers get translated into detailed action plans throughout the company? Don't forget the buyers in the purchasing department. Today they are buying quantities of specific items for certain delivery dates. Are they the right items to support your business plans? What about the quantities? What about the dates? How do you know if these are right or wrong? And if they are wrong, you will have another decision from the last long-range planning meeting to cry about at the next meeting!

Poor Performance Measures

Our performance measures also contribute to the problem. They are by and large financially oriented and tempt poor operating performance. For example, we measure purchasing people on their purchase price variance—how much they are paying for products compared with a standard usually set at the start of the fiscal year. We pay lip service to other measures of purchasing performance. So purchasing people locate vendors with cheaper prices who deliver erratically, sometimes late and sometimes early. But there is rarely any vendor penalty for late or early delivery and never a penalty for the buyer, who gets a pat on the back for purchase price savings no matter *when* the vendor delivers. But there is a huge penalty to the business. If the vendor is late, all other items purchased or made on time are held up. Excess inventories build, the factory is disrupted, and everyone tries to compensate for the late delivery with expediting, and disturbed schedules. Customers receive products late or warehouses go out of stock and lose sales. If the vendor is early, the result is excess inventory! And still the buyer gets a pat on the back—instead of a swift kick where it is deserved.

It is ridiculous to measure purchasing people on purchase price variance and not on delivery performance. It is a credit to the people in purchasing that they take it upon themselves to try to get products delivered on time. But when push comes to shove, they will perform to the financial measures, and the operating performance will suffer.

Another example of performance measures is the emphasis placed, in manufacturing, on efficiency and standard direct labor hours charged in a month. These are both financial measures, reported regularly each month and reviewed at high levels. Both of them tempt poor operating performance. Supervisors will overrun the required batch quantity at every opportunity, especially if the process is running well. They will keep large piles of work in their areas so they can pick and choose the ones they want to run. That's inventory! Plant managers will schedule production of items not needed but easy to make, especially near the end of the month, if they have not absorbed enough overhead. There is no penalty for making the wrong things, just a pat on the back for making many things productively. These are all ways of getting the lowest-cost obsolete inventory in the world!

The other side of the coin is inconsistency when it comes to controls, financial or operating. Plant managers are not authorized to buy capital equipment costing more than a relatively low figure, say $5000, without approval of the capital appropriations committee. Inventory planners, buyers, and supervisors have no such controls. They can easily commit $200,000 of company assets, or more, either to vendors or to production schedules. But these are the same assets. One is controlled tightly, even though recommended by a high-level manager, and the others are uncontrolled, even though authorized at much lower levels in the organization.

When you look at the dollars flowing the situation is even more ridiculous. Annual capital appropriations for a business are rarely more than a small percentage of the annual sales volume. But appropriations for materials and production schedule decisions, when you include direct factory overhead, are closer to 50 percent of annual sales. The thousands of decisions made daily that affect buying or production—such as when to schedule overtime, what parts to make, what materials to buy, how much to buy, and when to buy it—are not under control. And it is this phenomenon of huge amounts of capital committed by manufacturers and distributors without adequate controls that is disturbing the economy.

A *Wall Street Journal* article in 1976 had the headline "Under

Control. Inventory Managers Expect to Avert the Woes of Their 1974 Debacle." (The date—1974—refers to the last major boom-and-bust cycle.) The article stated that "inventory managers in most major corporations have been trying especially hard to keep inventories in line with sales, but inventories aren't always where you want them when you want them." This suggests to me that these companies implemented new specific controls after 1974 with the primary objective of controlling inventories.

But I refute their claim. Most manufacturers and distributors are no more in control now than in 1974. If they were, I could not make my statements about uncontrolled buying and scheduling decisions. All that has happened is that more people are being more careful about their inventory decisions because of top management pressure. But actual controls? No way. There will be another major boom-and-bust cycle in the next few years because we don't have any more control now than we did in 1974. The minor cycles we have had since then are proof of the lack of control. Getting the *right* controls in place is the only way to avoid boom-and-bust cycles.

The Supply Chain

The industrial economy of a country or of the world can be shown as a series of concentric circles as in Figure 1-1. Relatively few companies produce raw materials, which are moved through higher and higher levels of manufacture and distribution. The final level is when end customers buy something for their own use, either as a consumer item or as an industrial product.

Information about end-customer demand passes from company to company—that is, from tier to tier. In the example in Figure 1-1, such information passes from the outside circle to the inner one. Information about the availability of items to support this demand passes in the opposite direction, from supplier to consumer.

Inventories are used, at least in theory, to provide products either to customers or to the next higher level in the supply chain when demand exceeds supply. Inventories also exist so that suppliers can make products efficiently in large lots rather than a few at a time as well as for a host of other reasons. It is the presence of inventories and their management that is confusing. Decisions to increase or decrease inventories made at one tier of the supply chain have an immediate effect on the demand seen by the lower tiers. Information about the real demand now gets distorted, and wrong decisions are made by suppliers. This misinformation ricochets through the economy, distorting the information even more.

The biggest culprits causing this phenomenon are manufacturers and distributors of industrial and complex consumer items, which are in the majority of cases hard-goods-oriented. They are the major culprits only because of the huge variety of such items and the large number of different parts and raw materials used in their manufacture, resulting in more lines of communication between more tiers of supply and between more companies in these tiers. Hence the opportunity for error is greatest. But *all* manufacturers and distributors contribute to the problem. The only question is to what degree?

We will study a single plant's activities and relations with adjoining tiers of industry to understand the problem and its solution. The logistics policies will be discussed one at a time to clarify individual influences. In actual operation these policies are all contributing to the problem at the same time, a synergism that is deadly.

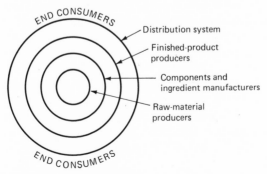

Fig. 1-1 Tiers of supply.

We will then consider linked factories and a multistage distribution system. The disturbance that inventory decisions cause will become very clear. The last step will be to show the effects on the total economy and how small changes in real demand are amplified through the logistics pipeline.

The tough job is to suggest how to combat the influences of inventory management on the total economy. It is possible, even mandatory, to solve the problem for a unique plant or business. It is even possible to insulate it from the worst of the external influences. But the total economy is another story.

Out of the solution for a plant must come the ability to capitalize on the problem and get *real* gains in market share. This ability will only be developed if you get a clear grip on currently uncontrolled decisions and have a full understanding of the strengths and weaknesses of logistics systems. And the economy will be under control only when enough companies adopt the right control mechanisms for their survival.

Chapter Two
The Lead-Time Syndrome

We might as well jump right into a phenomenon that has been going on for years: the lead-time syndrome. It is known by most inventory practitioners and purchasing people, yet few are doing anything to solve it. By itself the lead-time syndrome is a critical disturber of the industrial sector of our economy. But because of its ramifications, lead time is a major contributor to the amplification of small real-demand changes into large, but largely false, changes in order-flow rates and backlogs.

The term "lead time" means, in a broad sense, the length of time between placing an order for something and its actual receipt. To an inventory replenishment system lead time is the trigger that starts replenishment orders. Lead time operates the same whether the item is purchased from a vendor or made inside the plant. Lead times are also used to inform customers when they must place orders to expect receipt on time. It is a simple time-offsetting device. If we need something in week 10 and the lead time is 6 weeks, then the order must be placed by week 4 to expect on-time delivery. If the lead time is changed to 8 weeks, and we still need the item in week 10, the order must be placed by week 2.

Lead times are always changing, especially between buyer and seller. Why? If a manufacturer can make something in 6 weeks, why can't it always be made in 6 weeks? The reason is very simple: The manufacturer is being honest about lead times. But here is one place where honesty doesn't pay. It makes the problem worse.

The Demonstration Kit

Several years ago I developed, in conjunction with my associate George Plossl, a demonstration kit to show this lead-time syndrome. It simulates a business relationship between a vendor and his or her customers and the decisions that are made based on the information available. Capital equipment is purchased, plant expansions begun, and work-force changes made. The tragedy is these decisions are all wrong and triggered by "honest" lead times.

The kit simulates 4 customers buying products from the same sole-source vendor. Each customer wants 1 order of product per week from the vendor, each order an equivalent amount of vendor capacity but composed of different items. The customers buy other products from other vendors which they then use in conjunction with items from the sole-source vendor to make their products. We study only the sole-source vendor and the sole-source vendor's customers. The lead time for the vendor's products is 3 weeks. The vendor's capacity is 4 orders of products per week, again assuming equivalent vendor capacity in each order. With 4 customers each buying 1 order per week and a vendor capacity of 4 orders per week we have a nicely balanced system.

A competitive situation exists between the 4 customers. They are each trying to get the most products delivered on time from the vendor. Their penalty for early delivery from the vendor is 10 points per order per week early, the penalty simulating excess inventory, cash flow, and maybe storage space problems. The penalty for late delivery is 25 points per order per week late, charged because factory schedules are disrupted, because there may be customer service problems, and because the items received on time from other vendors become excess inventory that cannot be used. In the real world, the penalty for a late delivery from a vendor is always considered to be far higher than for an early one. In the demonstration kit the ratio is 2½ to 1, but in real life it is probably closer to 10 to 1 or even more.

Each customer has an identical tally sheet, one of which is shown in Figure 2-1. The tally sheet defines the schedule of receipts this customer wants and has room to record what actually happens. It is a very complicated system. The first column, "order number," is simply the number incrementally assigned to each needed delivery. It is the same as the week each order is scheduled to be received, column 3. In other words, order 1 is required in week 1, order 2 is required week 2, and so on. Is everyone still with me? Column 2 records the week each order was placed. This column has already been completed for the first three needed deliveries because of the vendor's initial lead time of 3 weeks. Order 1 needed in week 1 was ordered 3 weeks ago. Order 2 needed in week 2 was ordered 2 weeks ago, and order 3 was ordered 1 week ago or last week. This column will be completed as the demonstration progresses for the other orders with the actual week each order is placed. Column 4 records when the order is actually received

Order no.	Week no.			Early	Late	Order no.	Week no.			Early	Late
	Ord	Sched	Rec'd				Ord	Sched	Rec'd		
1	−3	1				18		18			
2	−2	2				19		19			
3	−1	3				20		20			
4		4				21		21			
5		5				22		22			
6		6				23		23			
7		7				24		24			
8		8				25		25			
9		9				26		26			
10		10				27		27			
11		11				28		28			
12		12				29		29			
13		13				30		30			
14		14				31		31			
15		15				32		32			
16		16				33		33			
17		17				34		34			

Fig. 2-1 Blue customer's tally sheet.

from the vendor. If on time, as measured against the scheduled due date from column 3, no penalties are recorded in the early and late columns. If early, 10 points are recorded in the early column, and if late, 25 points in the late column. The winner is the one with the smallest number of penalty points.

The customers have only one rule which they cannot violate. They must be covered by orders to the vendor at least to the quoted lead time. In other words, if the vendor changes the lead time from 3 to 6 weeks, all deliveries needed in the next 6 weeks must be ordered. The customers can release orders beyond the quoted lead time if they want to, but not for a shorter period of time. This is the way most customer-vendor relations are structured.

Each customer receives a deck of cards corresponding to the orders he or she needs. The cards perform a dual role: If given to the vendor, they are a released purchase order for delivery on the date scheduled; if the vendor returns a card to a customer, it is the receipt document or packing slip signifying actual delivery of the products ordered. The vendor already has the first three cards for orders 1 to 3 from each customer because they were placed on the basis of the initial 3-week quoted lead time.

The vendor has a tally sheet shown in Figure 2-2 that keeps track of the flow of orders from and shipments to customers.

Week no.	Capacity	New orders	Shipments	Backlog	Quoted lead time
Start	4	—	—	12	3

Fig. 2-2 Vendor's tally sheet for starting week.

Column 1 is the week number of the demonstration. Column 2 is the capacity of the vendor's facility, filled in for the start week as 4 orders per week. Column 3 will record the sum of new orders placed by the four customers each week. The vendor only makes to order, not to stock, so column 4, "shipments," will always be the same as "capacity," column 2. Column 5, "backlog," is filled in for the start week as 12 orders, three from each of four customers. ("Backlog" in this context is order book or portfolio, not late orders as in some countries.) It will be calculated as the game progresses from the backlog in the prior week, plus new orders received this week, minus shipments made this week, to give the resulting backlog this week. Column 6 is also calculated. It is the lead time the vendor quotes for the following week and is calculated by dividing the vendor's backlog this week by his or her capacity this week to give the quoted lead time for next week. In the start week it is still 3 weeks because 12 orders backlog divided by 4 orders capacity per week means new orders can be delivered in 3 weeks.

This calculation is a crucial one to understand. It is used by almost all manufacturers as the way to communicate information about delivery dates to their customers. It is also crucial to understand, as the demonstration progresses, that capacity changes are not made quickly, nor are they made without good reason. Capacity changes cost money. Hiring new personnel, subcontracting, scheduling overtime, and buying new equipment and better tooling are the major ways of increasing capacity. All are costly, and all take time to implement. They are not entered into lightly.

The vendor has only one rule which cannot be violated. An "honest" lead time must be quoted. In other words the lead time must be long enough to supply products on time. This "honest" lead time will always be calculated from backlog and capacity.

The vendor receives no penalties for late or early deliveries. Only customers register penalties. Again, as mentioned in the preface, this is the real world. Few buying-selling arrangements based on delivery reliability contain penalty clauses for the vendor.

A Typical Demonstration

The best way of understanding the lead-time syndrome is to actually take part in the demonstration. This is how the kit was designed, to be played by a group of people interested in understanding the phenomenon of changing lead times. Twenty people is an ideal-size group. Since we cannot actually play the game here I will describe a typical demonstration.

The players are broken up into four equal teams. Each team is a customer and is known by a color. Color-coded cards, name tags, rules, pens, and tally sheets help to keep the demonstration clear.

The vendor is always the person or persons conducting the demonstration. It's a little easier with two people sharing the vendor's role to keep track of what week you are in, to pickup and deliver cards, and to maintain the vendor's tally sheet accurately.

A blackboard or flipchart is used to record the current game week, what the vendor's quoted lead time is this week, and the minimum order coverage week, this week plus the quoted lead time.

To simplify this description we will assume customers only place orders for the minimum they are allowed. In real demonstrations, orders are often released sooner than this minimum, because of the penalty ratio between early and late deliveries. This is also true in the real world.

Week 1 arrives. The quoted lead time is 3 weeks, so the minimum coverage week is week 4. Customers are only covered with orders on the vendor through week 3, so each customer places one order.

The vendor makes and delivers four orders in week 1. His tally sheet shows for week 1 that his capacity is 4, new orders received were 4, shipments were 4, calculated backlog is still 12, and the lead time he can quote for orders received in week 2 is still 3. The customer tally sheets show order 4 placed on the vendor in week 1, order 1 received exactly on time in week 1, so no penalties. Only the vendor's tally sheet will be shown as it is the crucial one to understand. Week 2 is a repeat of

Week no.	Capacity	New orders	Shipments	Backlog	Quoted lead time
Start	4	—	—	12	3
1	4	4	4	12	3

Fig. 2-3 Vendor's tally sheet for start to week 1.

week 1. The minimum coverage moves out a week to week 5, 4 orders are placed, 4 are delivered, backlog and lead time stay constant. All deliveries are exactly on time, no penalties to any customer. Isn't this exciting?

Week no.	Capacity	New orders	Shipments	Backlog	Quoted lead time
1	4	4	4	12	3
2	4	4	4	12	3

Fig. 2-4 Vendor's tally sheet for week 1 to week 2.

Week 3 is a different story. I told you earlier that all tally sheets were identical. That wasn't quite true. Three are identical to Figure 2-1. One is different, as shown in Figure 2-5. One customer, the red team, needs one order every week just like the others, but also needs one extra order in week 6, the joker. You can see now that playing cards were used to design the demonstration.

The lead time is 3 weeks. Hence the joker and the four regular orders needed in week 6 are all released to the vendor

Order no.	Ord	Sched	Rec'd	Early	Late	Order no.	Ord	Sched	Rec'd	Early	Late
1	−3	1				18		18			
2	−2	2				19		19			
3	−1	3				20		20			
4		4				21		21			
5		5				22		22			
6		6				23		23			
Joker		6				24		24			
7		7				25		25			
8		8				26		26			
9		9				27		27			
10		10				28		28			
11		11				29		29			
12		12				30		30			
13		13				31		31			
14		14				32		32			
15		15				33		33			
16		16				34		34			
17		17				35		35			

Fig. 2-5 Red customer's tally sheet.

in week 3. The vendor's tally sheet shows capacity of 4, new orders received 5, shipments 4, and calculated backlog 13. Obviously 13 orders of backlog divided by 4 orders capacity means the lead time can no longer be 3. Before you mathematicians tell me it should be 3¼, it is important to know that vendors deal in increments of whole weeks only. I have never seen a vendor quote 3¼ weeks lead time. It could be worse. Data processing people quote in increments of "man years" and get away with it! "Weeks" is tame in comparison. So the lead time applying to orders placed in week 4 goes out to 4 weeks. No delivery penalties occurred in week 3. Each customer received his or her one order on time.

Week no.	Capacity	New orders	Shipments	Backlog	Quoted lead time
Start	4	—	—	12	3
1	4	4	4	12	3
2	4	4	4	12	3
3	4	5	4	13	4

Fig. 2-6 Vendor's tally sheet for start to week 3.

In week 4, with the quoted lead time of 4 weeks, the minimum coverage is week 8. But the customers are only covered through week 6. Each must now release two orders for weeks 7 and 8. This is a critical point. The regular order for week 7 has to be placed because 1 week passed. The additional order for delivery in week 8 is triggered because the lead time was lengthened from 3 weeks to 4.

The vendor's tally sheet for week 4 reads capacity 4, new orders 8, shipments 4, calculated backlog 17, and calculated lead time, rounded upward, 5 weeks. All deliveries to customers were on time, so no penalties.

Week no.	Capacity	New orders	Shipments	Backlog	Quoted lead time
3	4	5	4	13	4
4	4	8	4	17	5

Fig. 2-7 Vendor's tally sheet for weeks 3 and 4.

Week 5 is a repeat of week 4. The extra 1-week lead time triggers one order from each customer, the week passing triggers the regular order, so incoming orders are 8, shipments 4, backlog now 21. At this point the vendor reviews the situation. Since incoming orders are increasing and backlog is growing, the vendor comes to the conclusion that "business is picking up." The sales manager is quick to agree, "We're gaining market share." But what to do about these lead times? Increasing them 1 week at a time is not solving the problem of the pickup in business. After much deliberation the vendor decides to jump the lead time to get ahead of the incoming business. He quotes 8 weeks, applicable to week 6 order receipts. The minimum coverage week is therefore week 14.

Week no.	Capacity	New orders	Shipments	Backlog	Quoted lead time
4	4	8	4	17	5
5	4	8	4	21	8

Fig. 2-8 Vendor's tally sheet for weeks 4 and 5.

When this information is written on the blackboard, the first signs of uneasiness appear in the customer teams. Up to this point they are usually only mildly interested in the lead-time changes. But when the jump is made from 5 weeks to 8, they begin to fear not getting products from the vendor on time.

Remember the penalty ratio? In most demonstrations at least one team, frequently all teams, now starts releasing orders for deliveries even further out than week 14. It would be hard to find a more illogical reaction. When the vendor quotes 8 weeks lead time, they get concerned about deliveries arriving on time. As a result, they release orders further out, in fact an inferred vendor lead time of even more than 8 weeks. How can this be the solution?

Some teams also start overriding the scheduled delivery dates of their orders. They tell the vendor they want them earlier, for example, "I want order 14 delivered in week 12, not in week 14," and so on. That penalty ratio is a powerful influence. So in week 6, the vendor tally sheet reads capacity 4, new orders received 16, assuming only minimum coverage, and there is great jubilation in the vendor's sales department. Maybe the sales manager can start flying first class again now that all this extra business is coming in.

The reaction to the sudden surge in orders is "I'm glad we changed the lead time last week to 8 weeks. It was just in time! If we hadn't changed, we would have been murdered!" But now what to do in week 6? Shipments are 4, backlog climbs to 33 orders, and the lead time of 8 weeks is no longer valid. It is jumped to 12 weeks.

The lead times are jumped in the demonstration to cram the relatively long period of time it takes in the real world to escalate lead times into a few weeks. This speeds up the demonstration but does not diminish the critical point. And in some cases even the real world of manufacturing and distribution experiences these sudden surges, as we shall see later.

In week 6 another decision point is reached. The vendor capacity is four, but orders scheduled for delivery are five, the four regular orders plus the joker. "How can this happen?" someone might ask. "Doesn't the vendor know the company's capacity? Why didn't the vendor promise only what could be made?" There are a variety of answers to these questions. The first is that the vendor was using lead time as the control mechanism on order receipts, not capacity, so it was not considered. This is not an unusual condition in business because of the costs of adjusting capacity. The second answer is that few companies really know their capacity, so they often take orders and gamble they can ship on time. They rarely do. Still others know their capacity but are willing to lie to their customers to get the orders. They feel delivering late is better than not getting the order. And still others are pushed to take the orders by their customers even though both parties know the chances of shipping the products on time are slim to none. Defense contracts are notorious for this practice.

If you are in none of these categories, God bless you. Then why else are you delivering products with such poor customer service? Why do you have all this inventory but can't ship on time? Don't tell me it's because your vendors are late. The chances are you are the culprit.

So a choice has to be made as to which four orders out of the five promised will be delivered. It is an arbitrary decision in the demonstration, but I am sure you could think of all kinds of good reasons to make this decision in the real world. You have a cousin who works in one of the customers' purchasing departments, so that customer gets an order. And of course we always look after our biggest customers first. That is the red team, the ones who gave us the joker. So they get their two orders. That only leaves one order that can be made, but you have demand for two orders. You may select the reason for picking which one of the two to make!

Three customers get their deliveries on time, and one gets nothing. Additional concern builds in the left-out customer about receiving late deliveries, so she releases more orders and schedules them all earlier than their required dates, and the demonstration goes really crazy. You can see now why it is best to assign two people to represent the vendor, since there is so much happening. I will continue to describe the action, assuming minimum coverage only.

Week no.	Capacity	New orders	Shipments	Backlog	Quoted lead time
5	4	8	4	21	8
6	4	16	4	33	12

Fig. 2-9 Vendor's tally sheet for weeks 5 and 6.

In week 7, incoming orders are 20, shipments are still 4, and backlog increases to 49, so lead time is jumped to 20 weeks. Customer requirements are still five, the four needed this week plus the one unshippped from last week, so an arbitrary choice is made again of which four to deliver. Assuming that one of these orders is the one not shipped last week, then the first penalty points occur for late delivery.

Week no.	Capacity	New orders	Shipments	Backlog	Quoted lead time
6	4	16	4	33	12
7	4	20	4	49	20

Fig. 2-10 Vendor's tally sheet for weeks 6 and 7

Weeks 8, 9, and 10 are simply repeats of week 7, with incoming orders far in excess of shipments, backlog growing and lead times jumped to get ahead of the incoming orders.

Week no.	Capacity	New orders	Shipments	Backlog	Quoted lead time
7	4	20	4	49	20
8	4	36	4	81	30
9	4	44	4	121	40
10	4	44	4	161	40

Fig. 2-11   Vendor's tally sheet for weeks 7 to 10.

In week 10 the backlog has reached 161 orders, the lead time is out to 40 weeks, and the vendor decides to reconsider the situation. Looking at the incoming orders and large "healthy" backlog, he decides capacity is the problem. He definitely needs a lot more capacity. This week he received 44 orders with a capacity of only 4. Obviously a new plant is needed.

Someone at this stage will tell me, "No way! He should have time-phased the orders. That way he would have seen the demand is only 4 every week except for 5 in week 6." You are theoretically correct. As a matter of fact, there is a sheet in the demonstration game to help you do this. But don't forget that as the customers get nervous about receiving late deliveries, they move the scheduled dates on the orders earlier. Now the time-phased demand looks like a real growth in business, and a significant one at that.

So the vendor calls a special stockholders' meeting to discuss the situation and request approval to expand. He gives all the stockholders glowing reports of the large healthy backlog, how they are obviously gaining market share from the competition, and how everything looks great for the company. He receives approval to borrow the financing needed for the expansion.

The vendor also decides to squeeze more capacity out of the existing plant. With some additional tooling and by scheduling overtime he can get 5 orders per week output starting in week 11. This is obviously not enough with 44 incoming orders so he is also trying to locate a site for a new plant. The plant manager of the new factory wants to live in the Carolinas, so that's where it will be located. Now the only question is how to justify the Carolinas as the best location!

The vendor takes the large healthy backlog with him to see the bank manager, and she is very impressed. Obviously there is no risk lending this vendor money with his capacity sold out almost a year and incoming orders 11 times his capacity. So the vendor increases his debt at prevailing interest rates and is happy. The bank manager just lent a large sum of money to a "sure thing" at a good rate of interest, so she's happy. We shall see later whether they stay happy.

With capacity increasing to 5 orders per week in week 11, the vendor decides not to increase lead times in week 10 but hold them at 40 weeks. Is this honest? Sure it is. Calculate the numbers yourself. So in week 11, the tally sheet reads capacity 5, new orders 4, shipments 5 and backlog 160. Is it clear why only 4 orders were placed in week 11? The lead time did not change this week from last, so no orders were triggered by lead-time changes. The only orders triggered are because 1 week passed.

The vendor thinks "It must be the post office. They're holding up all my orders. I must write to my representative about the terrible mail service we get."

But what to do about the lead time? With a backlog of 160 and a capacity of 5, an honest lead time would be 32. He decides to wait. Obviously the 4 orders received is only a 1-week aberration. He's bound to get a lot more orders in the next few weeks. So he decides to hold at 40. Besides, he is busy with the new plant layout. Yesterday they held the ground-breaking ceremonies.

Week no.	Capacity	New orders	Shipments	Backlog	Quoted lead time
10	4	44	4	161	40
11	5	4	5	160	40

Fig. 2-12 Vendor's tally sheet for weeks 10 and 11.

Weeks 12 through 16 are a repeat of week 11. Four orders are received, 5 are shipped, backlog drops by 1 and lead time is held at 40. It's obvious that customers are now getting

Week no.	Capacity	New orders	Shipments	Backlog	Quoted lead time
11	5	4	5	160	40
12	5	4	5	159	40
13	5	4	5	158	40
14	5	4	5	157	40
15	5	4	5	156	40
16	5	4	5	155	

Fig. 2-13 Vendor's tally sheet for weeks 11 to 16.

penalty points for early deliveries but no one refuses them. They remain too concerned about late penalties.

The vendor is now dragged away from that fun endeavor, building a new plant, by the conditions at the old one. He sees the drop off in orders, the steady erosion of backlog, and questions why it is happening. The sales manager tells him, "We're losing market share! It's those long lead times. My customers are buying from someone else."

So the vendor decides to regain his lost business by giving the customers better service. The sales department quickly advertises their shorter lead times. Yes, you're right, they decide to cut them to 31 weeks, honest with 155 backlog and 5 capacity.

How many orders are received in week 17? Zero? If he's lucky, he gets zero. What actually happens is customers cancel orders. They have been getting early deliveries recently, so inventories and penalties are piling up. They want to reduce their exposure. So in week 17 with capacity 5, new orders are −32. This comes from a 9-week reduction in lead time, but 1 week having passed. So 8 weeks of orders can be cancelled and they are. Shipments are 5 and backlog drops to 118. The vendor's reaction: "That didn't work. Let's try it again." So lead times are cut again, this time to 24 weeks.

Week no.	Capacity	New orders	Shipments	Backlog	Quoted lead time
16	5	4	5	155	31
17	5	−32	5	118	24

Fig. 2-14 Vendor's tally sheet for weeks 16 and 17.

In weeks 18 through 22, the combination of order cancellations and shipping at 5 orders per week reduces backlogs to 13 orders. The vendor reevaluates the situation and is convinced he is in a recession. The flow rate of new orders is negative and has been for several weeks. Backlogs have dropped to 13 orders, less than 3 weeks production at the current rate. The *Wall Street Journal, Business Week,* and other magazines are all warning we are in a recession.

It is obvious he has too much capacity. And in conditions of recession you must have a defensive business strategy. So he shuts off the overtime, lays off 25 percent of the work force, and reduces capacity to 3 orders per week. Construction on the new plant is immediately halted.

Week no.	Capacity	New orders	Shipments	Backlog	Quoted lead time
17	5	−32	5	118	24
18	5	−24	5	89	18
19	5	−20	5	64	13
20	5	−16	5	43	9
21	5	−12	5	26	6
22	5	− 8	5	13	3
23	3				

Fig. 2-15 Vendor's tally sheet for weeks 17 to 23.

He pays another visit to the bank manager. This time he explains he will not be able to make the payments on the loan with shipments at 3 per week when he was planning they would be 5. The bank manager looks with concern at the order cancellations and erosion of backlog. She agrees to extend the loan to reduce the payments but demands collateral in the form of chattel mortgages on the existing plant and machinery. Debt financing now becomes a huge drain on the company's profits and cash flow.

A special stockholders' meeting is scheduled by a few influential stockholders. Just a few months ago they had glowing reports from the management of how their money was safe. Not only that, but predictions of high rates of return on their money after the new plant came on stream. And of course, real appreciation in the value of their stock. Now they are facing losses, with a half-built plant and a large part of their work force on layoff. There is serious concern about the ability of this management team to run the show. A majority of stockholders call for the resignation of the general manager and key members of the staff.

Can It Get Any Worse?

I hate to tell you this, but we have only just started. I described only one element of the lead-time syndrome. Let's look at another which I will call the "triple-forecasting problem."

Every order placed from a customer to a vendor is three forecasts. When you place an order with a vendor, you forecast which item you will need (and you're wrong), how many you will need (wrong again), and when you will need them (wrong the third time). The degree of error depends on many factors. The major one is how far ahead of time you make the forecast. Forecasts are always more wrong the further ahead of time they are made. This can be represented by the trumpet shape of Figure 2-16.

What makes orders get placed further ahead of time? Our old "friend," lead time—the trigger mechanism in the inventory replenishment system that forces release of an order sometime prior to its need.

The same comment about forecast errors applies just as much to factory orders as to purchase or sales orders. The only difference is internal manufacturing lead times are rarely allowed to get as ridiculously out of hand as external lead times. But a factory or shop order is also three forecasts, all wrong to some degree. The degree again is largely dependent on the lead time in the inventory replenishment system.

We bring this element into the demonstration with a specially made six-sided die. It is marked with the numbers +3 through −3, and is used when the quoted lead time from the vendor exceeds 8 weeks. At this point, arbitrarily chosen, we say the error in the three forecasts is getting high, especially the time of need. So after the lead time reaches 8 weeks, just before deliveries are made, the die is rolled. Its number is the random adjustment of the scheduled due date. In other words, when

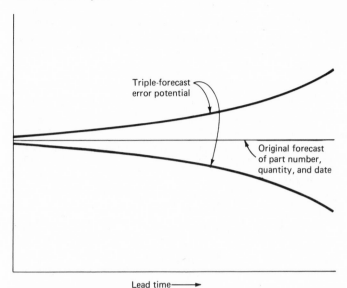

Triple-forecast
error potential

Original forecast
of part number,
quantity, and date

Lead time⟶

Fig. 2-16 Triple-forecast error problem.

the customer placed the order for delivery in a certain week, her forecast was wrong by the number on the die. This is marked on the tally sheet by changing the scheduled due date by the die number. Actual deliveries are now compared to the revised due date to calculate penalty points.

You can imagine what happens next. Penalty points start escalating rapidly, the customer teams start trying to outfox the die and the vendor, but there is no way to do that, at least no way that works. The combination of the vendor's arbitrarily deciding to whom the orders should be delivered and the randomness of the cast of the die means the customers have no control. A feeling of great frustration builds up in the customer teams.

The Real World?

It's always interesting to consider how closely this simple demonstration simulates reality. Does the lead-time syndrome really happen in real life? If the reports from at least 75 percent of those attending these demonstrations are any gauge, it is remarkably true to life. Many of them recall recent experiences where orders, backlogs, and capacity changes were all the result of lead-time changes. The sad part is they feel resigned to its effects. They either believe that lead-time changes cannot be overcome and therefore they must resign themselves to being its victim, or they feel that only if all customers of a given vendor are cooperating can the syndrome be stopped. Neither of these opinions is fact. The syndrome *can* be cured for one customer working with one vendor. There is no question that the total economy needs a more aggregate approach to isolate it from these effects, but let's not wait for that to develop. I'm not sure it ever will, and neither am I sure it's desirable. Some of the planned economies of the world have even worse problems than ours.

It's also a fact that many products regularly oscillate between relatively short and very long lead times. Bearings, resistors, capacitors, integrated circuits, glass bottles, forgings, castings, and a myriad of other products have all experienced this phenomenon in the past few years and will again. We can blame inflation, the oil crisis, fluctuating exchange rates, or the actions of the Federal Reserve Board, but none of those is the culprit. Oh yes, one of those *could* cause the joker. But the joker is only the trigger mechanism of the syndrome. The rest is caused by logistics systems, salespeople, purchasing agents, and even general managers who either don't know how to control it or refuse to accept that it should be controlled. Those big healthy backlogs make people feel comfortable.

But there is no such thing as a "big healthy backlog." A big backlog means the lead-time syndrome is operating, and the only question is when the cancellations will start. Even custom builders should look at large backlogs with concern. Cancellation penalties built into the contract won't stop cancellations. And the same cycle of expanding and contracting capacity to suit the changing backlogs is still not a very efficient way of running a business.

The demonstration does *not* simulate the real world very well. It is much too simple. Most vendors have hundreds of customers. They also have a wide product range with sales fluctuating up and down between product families all the time. It is very hard to sort out real demand from fictitious demand in this situation.

The customer demand is constant in the demonstration, set at one order every week from each customer plus the joker. But what if the customers are also subject to the lead-time syndrome? What if they are changing lead times to their customers? Then the flow rate of orders they get will vary and be transferred to the vendor as increased demands, not level demands each week.

And finally, the demonstration has a sole-source vendor. Most companies have either multiple vendors or multiple sources of supply, for example, from factory or warehouse. In this environment, double-ordering from two or more sources becomes commonplace to guarantee that materials are available. A huge false impact on the economy is the result. Never forget that purchasing people only get fired if the factory is short of materials and shuts down or the distributor is out of stock of key items. They never get fired for having too much!

The syndrome is so insidious that its effects can be caused without actually changing the quoted lead time. A client of mine has a central metalware factory supplying metal, plastic, and other components to several assembly plants. By corporate policy, the lead time for all items coming from metalware is 14 weeks. It never changes. But the information grapevine between the plants is a very powerful medium. A casual comment is made about the capacity of the metalware factory being tight, maybe because they received a joker. Immediately all assembly plants release more work for components "to get their place in the queue." There's that biased penalty system at work.

Metalware receives this huge influx of business, which is obviously not false because they didn't change their quoted lead times. So they hire people, work extensive overtime, arrange to add machinery, subcontract work outside, and for a few months are very busy.

Then something funny happens. The inflow of new orders dries up, backlogs drop, and the problem now is how to get rid of the excess capacity. Overtime is shut off and all subcontract work is pulled back into the plant. But that's not enough, so skilled metalware people are farmed out to whatever jobs are available or, in the bad times, laid off.

If you look at a year's production, it comes remarkably close to the predictions of need the assembly plants provide each year and the total they order. So the total demand is stable. But the actual orders are a far cry from being stable. The cost and social impact of the activities caused by this mechanism are horrendous.

This proves the existence of another philosophy at work which I will label "shortage emotion." People who plan, schedule, and manage inventories have an extreme bias about their problems. The worst is being out of stock. Being out of stock is the most heinous crime of inventory management. Having excess is low on the problem scale. The penalty point distribution between late deliveries versus early ones exemplifies this bias. So anytime there is a fear of not getting deliveries early enough, more is ordered sooner. And this is done regardless of the details in the inventory system. People override these details to ensure "they are covered." We will refer to this again later. I hope you see what more, sooner means: jokers for the vendors and eventually, of course, excess inventory.

So, is the demonstration representative of the real world? No way! The real world is far more complex. But the demonstration does show the impact of lead-time changes on the flow rates of orders, and that is certainly a part of the real world. Clearly lead-time changes are an event to be watched for and controlled.

A Complete Understanding

Let's evaluate what happened between customer and vendor in the demonstration and see what other influences could be at work.

It is clear that the flow rate of new orders was totally

unrelated to demand. The real demand was four orders every week throughout the demonstration horizon plus one, the joker. But where do you see that on the vendor's tally sheet? Nowhere! Order flows vary from 4 per week to 44 per week and then go negative when the cancellations start. How does this situation relate to real demand? It doesn't.

Backlogs vary from 12 orders to 161 orders and back down again. Does this variation show real demand? No again.

The closest correlation is shown in the shipments and capacity columns but the figures in these columns still don't match real demand. The vendor ignores the real demand of 5 orders in week 6 and then goes to a figure of 5 orders per week when the real demand is only 4. Of course when the crash comes, capacity and shipments are cut to 3 when demand is still 4.

We call this syndrome the "vicious cycle," shown in Figure 2-17. It occurs in almost every industry. A vendor gets a little more business in one week, realizes that the lead time is no longer valid, and quotes a longer lead time. The customers need materials at a certain rate to keep their plants operating, so they are forced to release orders earlier. The vendor sees

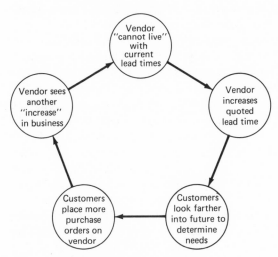

Fig. 2-17 Vicious purchasing cycle.

another apparent increase in business, lengthens the lead time again, and we're off and running.

Even businesses that quote delivery of each customer order separately, like the machine-tool or the computer industry, are not immune. As their backlogs of orders grow, customers who think they may buy a machine but are not yet ready to commit themselves are forced to place orders to reserve a place in queue. So the backlogs start growing with a lot of questionable demand, and we're into the lead-time syndrome again.

Sales agents are also great at starting this cycle. When they hear the plant is tight on capacity, they immediately go to their best customers, obviously the ones who buy the most, and tell them, "The plant is in trouble; we have a real capacity problem. Get your orders in now so I can protect your deliveries." And you can bet the plant is *now* in trouble.

Ms. Sales Manager or Mr. General Manager, please don't pay sales commissions on orders received. (Some companies do, you know.) What a wonderful way of paying people to start the lead-time syndrome. Pay after you receive the money from the customer. This won't stop the syndrome, but it sure won't be an incentive to start it.

Computers, those wonderful black boxes that are not an unmixed blessing, are great at helping people who don't understand this syndrome to aggravate it. Recently introduced software from a large computer hardware manufacturer has the lead-time syndrome built right in. And it seems so logical. The software is for finished goods management; hence it is a distribution-related system. It records the dates when orders are placed with vendors and when products are received. The difference in dates is obviously the actual lead time for these items. This actual lead time is compared to the planned lead time in the system by using weighted averages. The actual lead time modifies the planned lead time automatically. Can you imagine a more logical but more incorrect technique? They have succeeded in computerizing the lead-time syndrome. In defense of the software, this is an optional feature, not mandatory. But what a time bomb to have sitting in a software program just waiting for someone to activate it. And I bet a clerical person, untrained in the logistics field, is the one who can activate it in most cases. Here is one place where common sense is completely inadequate.

Purchasing magazines which carry a listing of the latest quoted lead times for commodity groupings are also set up to aggravate the situation. As most production and inventory control systems today are computerized, it is a simple matter to program the computer to change all lead times for a certain commodity. If they have increased, a pile of requisitions, or purchase orders, if the system is this automated, are printed for review the next day. Obviously all of this material is needed, otherwise the orders wouldn't have been printed. So into the mail goes the next slug of orders that will trigger the next lead-time increase. In the days of manual systems, changing lead times on all records and refiguring the release of orders could take several weeks. This system slowed down the pace of lead-time escalation. But today the change can be made and processed in a matter of days. This trend can do nothing but make matters worse. Of course the computer experts will tell us that we should have the customer's computers talking directly to the vendor's computers. This way we would go through the lead-time syndrome so fast we wouldn't know about it. But don't bet on it!

The key information used by many managers of manufacturing and distribution companies to evaluate the health of their business—order flows relative to shipments and backlogs—has been proved invalid. It does *not* measure the health of their businesses. It *does* measure what is happening to lead times and ultimately to inventories, which has little if anything to do with real business health.

The same information is used by economists and business writers to measure the health of the economy. This measurement is also invalid for the same reasons. Lead times are changing, not real demand.

Chapter Three

Invalid and Disruptive Concepts

The lead-time syndrome described in Chapter 2 is the first damaging influence of inventory systems on both business and the economy. The lengthening and shortening of lead times creates changes in the flow rates of orders and backlogs that are completely unrelated to real demand changes. More important, the lengthening of lead times forces ordering decisions to be made earlier and earlier, triggering the triple-forecast error problem. Thus order flows are not only unrelated to real demand, but they are for the wrong items. Any business seeing these fictitious orders cannot possibly sort out real demand from false. Poor decisions are the inevitable result.

There is also a key psychological factor here. A large part of our economy is influenced by the business and investment communities' perception of its health. Consumer spending is also influenced by this same perception, transmitted to the consumer by various news media. And two of the key economic indicators are both backlogs and order flows in relation to shipments. But these are false indicators that seriously distort the real facts. The actual change in inventories is minor in comparison to this effect. In the demonstration, backlogs and order flows changed by a factor of 10 to 15. Actual inventories in the customer plants changed by a much smaller amount. Although this smaller amount is still significant, especially since actual inventories consumed company cash to create so-called assets, they are not the major business and economic influence. Order flows and backlogs are.

The Waste of Resources

Let's now start to discuss the waste of resources caused by this syndrome. I won't cover the full waste of resources here because we have more immediate problems. Later chapters will give a much better account of the total impact. First I want to give you a flavor of the costs to prepare you for the worst to come.

Let's look at the demonstration again and see the vendor's costs. The vendor starts incurring these about week 6 when the lead time has reached 8 weeks. At this point in time, orders are placed for 2 months in the future. Two months in the future doesn't sound bad, does it? But how well can you predict what items you need and in what quantities you will need them for your production or sales at that future date? In most cases the answer is a fairly good prediction for some items and a poor prediction for others. Let's assume the customers make poor forecasts.

The customers place orders for these items 2 months before they are needed. One month goes by. The customers now evaluate the orders they placed 1 month ago against their latest forecasts. Lo and behold, they realize that some orders are for the wrong items, others are for the wrong quantities, and still others are for the wrong dates. If they are lucky, some will still be close. No problem. Just call the vendor and change the schedules to the latest prediction of need. I'll leave you to imagine what happens when forecasts are made 40 weeks or 10 months in the future.

So the inside sales force at the vendor's plant starts processing the customer's change orders, causing the production and inventory control people to start changing schedules. The vendor's purchasing department in turn starts changing schedules with their vendors because of different material needs.

This is all additional work, and comes from overtime, temporary help, new hires, or reassignments from other activities. Do you see the waste? Not one piece of this work is productive, just additional overhead costs, which aren't even necessary.

A visit I made to a new client will give you an understanding of how ridiculous the situation can get. Obviously I need a lot of background information before making any recommendations to new clients, so I spent a couple of days interviewing people involved in all aspects of the business. In addition to getting to know people, I am particularly interested in gauging the extent of their logistics knowledge.

The time finally came to visit the data processing manager. After the preliminaries of going to see the computer (when you've seen one, you've seen them all as far as I'm concerned), I asked him, "What are you doing to support manufacturing?" He replied, "Nothing. I'm busy because we just received a bigger computer. At the moment I'm going through the conversion cycle, and then we're going to implement our new order entry system." I asked, "On what basis and for what applications did you justify the large machine?" He answered, "To support order entry. We have 45 weeks of customer orders in backlog, which exceeds our current file capacity. And the number of changes we have to make to these orders based on customer requests takes too much time on the small machine. So we are now leasing a bigger machine which, with the new software programs, will allow us to have 100 weeks of orders."

No, he was not working in a machine-tool factory. The plant made metal film resistors. The actual lead time from start to finish of a resistor is a couple of weeks. But the lead-time syndrome had caused the large backlog, which exceeded the capacity of their customer-order file and resulted in their spending money and using scarce data processing resources to achieve nothing. To add insult to injury, before the new software programs were implemented, the factory's backlog had dropped to a more normal 4 weeks. Oh well, at least they will be ready the next time. And maybe they'll get around to doing something productive with their larger machine after it starts running.

The vendor incurs additional costs when capacity is changed in week 11. Overtime is scheduled, and we all know what this costs. Not only is a premium paid for the hours worked, but absenteeism rises, quality often suffers, and productivity drops. In the real world a higher percentage of overtime has to be scheduled to realize 25 percent more output. The vendor added tooling, a capital expense, with no return. And of course, the new plant costs were all for naught, including the debt costs.

When the bank manager was approached the second time, the debt costs went up, a part of the business was transferred to the bank's control and the vendor lost again. The cutback in capacity was costly. People get used to working overtime— or at least to a fatter paycheck each week. They come to rely on it. When overtime was stopped, discontent in the work force grew. Productivity slid again with everyone afraid of being laid off. Talk of union protection started. When the layoffs hit, this company was ripe for a successful union election.

And what's the return on a half-finished plant? Don't tell me zero. It's a very large negative return. How many times have you been in the vendor's shoes?

What about the customers? What are their additional costs? Up to about week 6, there are none. They process a few more purchase orders than normal, but this is not significant. But in week 6 one customer does not receive an order for needed material. We have talked earlier about the disruption this causes. From this point until week 11 customers regularly get some late deliveries. One order is late as a minimum every week. But don't forget the die. The forecasts of need as expressed by the submitted purchase orders are wrong. So although the bias is to late deliveries, early ones also occur. Inventories climb, the factory is disrupted, and their customers' schedules are upset. The clerical work involved in keeping in touch with the vendor and changing dates on orders is excess effort. Trying to keep the factory running by scheduling around the disruption is also excess effort. Again, not one piece of this is productive or necessary. Quite the contrary. How many times have you been one of these customers? And an even better question: How often have you been both vendor and customer at the same time? In the real world, aren't we all customers and vendors?

It is also interesting to evaluate the vendor's delivery performance first from the vendor's point of view and then from the customers' perspective. Up to week 6 he delivers 100 percent on time from both the customers' and vendor's viewpoint. In week 6 he delivers 1 order that is late according to the original schedule date. He delivers 1 order late each following week until week 11, when he delivers everything on time. At this point he has delivered 45 orders, 4 each week plus the joker. Five of them were late, 1 in each of the weeks 6 through 10. His average customer service over this period, based on the originally scheduled due dates, was 40 orders on time over a total of 45 or 89 percent on time. Not too bad.

But look at this from the customers' point of view. They are not interested in the original date for which they scheduled material, but on the revised date as dictated by the die. After week 6 the die starts rolling and few orders arrive on time. When orders are on time, it's by luck. So customers see no orders delivered on time; hence, they see the vendor in a poor light. The same situation looked at from two perspectives gives drastically different results. But, more important, both the customer and the vendor lose.

The Five Choices

Remember week 3? That's when the joker was placed, and suddenly 5 orders showed up against a capacity of 4. What were the choices at that time? There are 5. If you don't like the first one, you have 4 left, and so on. There are costs and problems associated with each one, but also benefits. The trick is to find the least bad choice.

The vendor selected choice one, which was to extend the lead time. In the real world the word "selected" is the wrong word to use. The vendor extended the lead time by default—by not considering any other possibilities. Extending the lead time seemed to be the logical thing to do. No one questioned whether it really was.

The costs and problems of this "solution" were well documented earlier. The key point to realize is it's no solution. In week 3, with a backlog of 13, there was 1 excess order, the joker. In week 4, there was still 1 excess order even though the backlog was 17. In every week there was 1 excess order, no matter what was done to the lead time. Only when capacity was added in week 11 did the excess order go away. But now the extra capacity was retained to eat up the huge backlog that shouldn't have been there to start with.

This leads us to an important law about lead times: Lead times will be what you say they are, plus sometimes a little bit more. In other words lead times trigger backlogs, and backlogs result in extended lead times so they both contribute to a vicious cycle. The real demand for most companies' products is relatively level. Some companies have highly seasonal demands and others have peaks and valleys, but these kinds of companies are fairly rare. In aggregate, the demand for most products is level. How else can your shipments be so even each month? So changing lead times triggers variations in this otherwise stable demand. The average demand doesn't change. The "plus sometimes a little bit more" is a joker. As we have found out, changing lead times to handle a joker doesn't work.

Capacity booking is another form of extending lead times. This term applies to those companies who set their capacity and simply book orders against each period's planned output. With capacity booking, when the 5 orders show up in week 3 for week 6 delivery, 4 are promised in week 6 and 1 in week 7. But 4 more orders show up in week 4 for week 7 delivery. Only 3 can be promised for delivery in week 7. One unit of capacity in week 7 was promised the prior week. So one gets bumped to week 8. But customers want their orders delivered when they asked for them, not 1 week late. The race is now on to see which customer can place orders early enough to get in the vendor's queue and be promised delivery when desired. The last customer to place an order gets bumped, and the bumped customer subsequently releases orders sooner than needed in order to secure a place in queue. The customers thus play leapfrog. They all get some orders late, so they pressure the vendor to add capacity, which finally occurs. This is not a satisfactory answer, but it is probably slightly better than changing lead times.

The second choice is to lie a lot. Don't change lead times, promise deliveries to customers when they want them, but, of course, with a capacity of 4 and with 5 orders received, some customer will not receive an order. This is the second most common strategy in industry today. It occurs for one of two reasons. Few companies know or will admit their real capacity. They feel it is more than it really is and so make promises based on this incorrect perception. Or they believe it is better to lie to the customer, get the order, and deliver late, than tell the truth and risk not getting the order at all.

As we discussed earlier, using the central metalware factory supplying parts to several assembly plants as an example, this won't work either. The grapevine of information flowing between customer and vendor as well as the real fact of late deliveries, will trigger orders to be placed by customers way ahead of time. Customers will request earlier deliveries to get in the early part of the vendor's queue and the whole process is started. The danger of lying a lot is you may enrage customers and lose their accounts. It would be better to lose one order from a company than their total business.

Choice three is to add capacity in weeks 3 through 6 to deliver 5 orders in week 6. In 3 weeks 12 orders are normally produced. With the joker, 13 are needed. This is just over 8 percent more capacity for each of 3 weeks, easily handled by overtime in most plants. If this had been done, the only cost penalty would have been the vendor's to pay for overtime. Customers would have received all their products on time, the lead time would have stayed constant at 3 weeks, and the backlog would remain stable at 12, apart from the 3 weeks that included the joker. No other changes would have occurred.

So why didn't the vendor change the capacity for weeks 3 to 6? The extra order is a capacity problem; therefore capacity is the only solution.

The answer lies in the normal information flow between

vendor and customer. It consists of pieces of paper called purchase orders and sales orders. These define an item, a quantity, and a delivery date. They do not provide a picture of future capacity required.

So in come the 4 regular orders plus the joker. Is the joker an incremental increase in business or simply a week 4 order placed in week 3? How does the vendor know? It's simple—he doesn't. So the obvious solution—now that we have seen the demonstration—is bypassed and the wrong solution chosen. And, you think, why not? Aren't big backlogs healthy, just as economists, business writers, and college professors have been telling us for years? And, you might reason, why spend money on overtime now, if it's simply an early release of an order, and have people idle next week? That's not smart business. Too much capacity was the reason we got hurt badly during the bust phase of the last business cycle. We don't want to fall into that trap again. We'll wait to be sure there has been a real pickup in business before we add capacity. This is exactly the thought process that leads to the bust trap you were trying to avoid in the first place!

The fourth choice is to refuse the extra order. Most people become paranoid when this is suggested, as if refusing orders were against their religion. But accepting orders is, or should be, a conscious decision. Refusing them should be also. But the tough job is knowing when to accept or refuse. As mentioned earlier, most plants don't know if the extra order is an incremental increase in business or simply an earlier release of a regular order.

But I hope we can at least agree that taking orders for delivery too far in the future is ridiculous. At least these orders should be refused. Maybe we could even establish a company policy to determine this cut-off point. The triple forecast error problem (including item, quantity, and date) at some point becomes too risky and must be avoided.

The problem is what to do after this cut-off point has been established. If the vendor opens the books to new orders every now and then, the customers who get their orders in soonest will eat up the capacity and take more than they need. Don't forget that the pressure is always on to be covered when you manage inventories, never to be caught short. This means other customers will get none. Later on, the customers who ordered too much will cancel or reschedule, leaving the vendor with excess capacity and a loss of business.

One way out of this dilemma is to allocate capacity to customers. The steel industry did this in 1974. Lead times for many types of steel had climbed to 12 months, and the steel companies were concerned about the reliability of these orders. They reduced the lead time to about 3 months and allocated capacity to customers beyond this time based on a percentage of their previous year's take. Each month, customers ordered the fourth month's production in specific items and quantities for delivery that month.

The steel industry was on the right track. The mistake they made was to allocate a percentage of capacity based on last year's take. And they also waited until the lead-time syndrome had been running for a while and shortage emotion had taken root. So everybody took their full allocation and cried for more, even though in many cases their allocation was more than they needed. So some companies had excess steel and others experienced real shortages.

Last year's take was a poor basis for setting the allocation policy. A black market for steel then started; it sold at a premium, but most companies bought all they could get. The black-market steel came from those companies who took their full allocation but didn't need it, as well as from the real excess capacity the steel industry had. Yes, that's right, even though lead times had climbed to a full year, there was excess capacity.

The "Buy it now in case you can't get it later" philosophy was the culprit. When the bubble burst, customers had so much inventory that the steel industry suffered for several years before this excess material was absorbed. Operating levels below 70 percent capacity were common, whereas in 1974 they were at over 90 percent capacity with preventive maintenance deferred to make more steel.

The fifth choice is to sell capacity long term and products short term. I don't mean when you are in the lead-time syndrome; I mean as a regular policy. This is sometimes called a "capacity contract."

The lead-time demonstration can be played four ways, all varying in degree of complexity. Two of the ways contain a capacity contract between one customer and the vendor. The contract, agreed to by both parties, is for the customer to place one order each week and for the vendor to supply one order each week. The lead time to define the specific items and quantities is always 3 weeks. The capacity contract extends as far as the vendor's quoted lead time to the other three customers.

Because this one customer only decides the specifics needed 3 weeks out, the triple-forecast error problem and the die do not apply to her orders. She always gets deliveries on time and thus incurs no penalties. She wins the competition every time. The other three customers get even more penalties because now the joker is one extra in three, not in four.

What if the vendor had this kind of contract with all four customers? What would have happened regarding the joker? The red customer would have realized she needed more product in a week than the contract stated. The vendor would have realized it was incremental demand, not an earlier release of the regular demand. He may even have known about it several weeks before week 3, depending on his future visibility of needs.

So the red customer would have had to negotiate with the vendor for the additional order of capacity before releasing the joker. The vendor, seeing the incremental nature of the order, would have added capacity to handle it or refused it if he was unable to change capacity. The lead-time syndrome could not have started.

Some people confuse this way of working with blanket orders. They are not the same. A "blanket order" defines a specific item and usually gives a schedule of quantities to be delivered at certain times. Sometimes these quantities and dates are for information only, not a schedule. The customer reserves the right to call off quantities and dates with a short lead time.

A capacity contract does not define item, quantity, or date. It defines capacity, or, to use a better term, the required flow rate. The specific makeup of item, quantity, and date is left completely open or defined within wide tolerances. The difference between the two is the higher degree of specificity on blanket orders versus capacity contracts.

So which of the five choices should one make? There's only one possible answer: the last choice. The capacity contract is the only sure way to beat the lead-time syndrome. But it is not an easy way of working. It depends on trust between vendor and customer, and is thus a highly people-oriented approach. But those few companies that have made the capacity contract work reap the benefits everyday.

Communication between customer and vendor about flow rates is a key to stopping false information from disturbing the economy. When there is good communication, demand changes do not result in unnecessary lead-time changes and false information is not generated. All tiers in the supply chain get quality information. So part of the solution to our economic boom-and-bust cycle is better flow-rate information. However, our current way of communicating between customer and vendor, by using sales and purchase orders, does not provide this necessary data. A completely new set of information must be developed and effectively used, and a new way of operating must be developed for all sales and purchasing people.

Is This the Whole Picture?

No, it's going to get worse. I have alluded a number of times to shortage emotion and how this affects our decisions. Would you believe we have other "logical" techniques teamed with the lead-time syndrome and shortage emotion to cause even more trouble? You bet we do. They will be the subject of the next chapter. Get ready for an even wilder roller-coaster ride.

Chapter Four
The Inventory Variables

The lead-time syndrome is only one of the disruptive elements in inventory systems that affect the economy. There are several more, all acting in concert with lead-time changes. The total impact is what we have to combat.

The lead-time syndrome by itself affects the information flow between customer and vendor. The order flow rate gets completely out of step with real demand. But it does not change the total demand. It simply causes release of orders earlier or later. Only when lead times get excessive and order forecasts are too far off, does the lead-time syndrome create extra demand to cover the shortages. Of course, when vendors decide to add capacity they put extra demand on their own vendors. When they construct buildings and buy machinery, all unnecessary, then extra demand is placed on these sources. The reverse also happens when capacity is reduced. But this extra demand occurs only as the result of extreme lead-time escalation or reduction. It does not occur during normal day-to-day business activities.

What if we had techniques and systems that automatically changed total demands routinely? Is that possible in today's technological world? Believe it or not, the answer is yes. And the system is very logical. The commodity that changes real demand is inventory. Almost any decision affecting inventory, other than to force it to be constant, will change the demands on the supplier of this inventory. If you plan to increase inventory, then your suppliers must make and deliver more than your usual demand. If you plan for it to decrease, the reverse must happen.

It is the ability of inventory to act as a modifier of demand that now becomes our concern. As we shall see later, all our inventory theory, systems, and emotions work to magnify small "end-customer" demand changes into huge supplier demand changes. The inventory variables are the jokers in the deck. Not only that, they are the seemingly logical, but actually illogical, amplifiers of demand.

Inventory Replenishment Systems

We must digress a moment to discuss inventory replenishment systems. I do not intend to make you an expert in inventory theory and techniques, but it's important to set the stage for the later discussion. If you are already familiar with the terms "order point" (OP), "material requirements planning" (MRP), "time-phased order point" (TPOP), and "distribution requirements planning" (DRP), you can skip this section. If you're not sure or don't understand these terms at all, please read on.

There are only two basic techniques to choose from to manage inventories. One is called order point and the other is called material requirements planning. Some features of each can be combined to create the time-phased order point, an integral part of distribution requirements planning. We will discuss each in turn to see their methodology.

"Order point" means simply that we establish a level of inventory for an item which, when reached, triggers a replenishment order. In its simplest form it's a line scratched on the inside of a storage bin. When inventories drop below this level, a replenishment order is issued. A more sophisticated method is to keep records, either manually or in a computer, of the on-hand inventory. A calculated order point is then compared regularly with the on-hand figure. When on-hand inventory drops below the order point, a replenishment order is triggered.

The formula to calculate an order point is

Order point = [period demand × lead time (periods)]
+ safety stock

The first part of the formula ensures we have enough inventory to cover average demand before the replenishment order arrives at the end of the lead time. But demand is rarely known accurately. In most cases when using order points it is a forecast based on past history. The safety stock portion of the equation provides contingency when actual demand exceeds what was predicted. Of course, if actual demand is less than what was forecasted, which it should be half the time if the forecast is reasonable, then safety stock is excess inventory half the time and of no value whatsoever. The order-point methodology is shown graphically in Figure 4-1.

Since this technique was developed formally around 1934, statisticians, mathematicians, and college professors have had

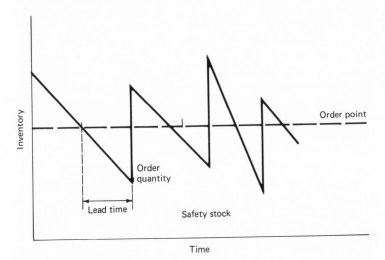

Fig. 4-1 Order point.

a field day. Finally they have an opportunity to apply proba-
bility theory and frequency distributions to the real world! No
more useless examples like predicting the height of the next
black-haired swimmer who will swim the English Channel!

We will not delve deeply into safety stock theory here. If
you need more information, there are some good references
in the bibliography. However it is important to know what is
considered in the theory. The variability of actual demand
from forecast is a factor; the lead time to replenish is a factor
(remember the triple-forecast error problem gets bigger the
further out you forecast); the lot size of replenishment is a
factor (if you replenish in annual lots you are protected against
stock-outs almost all year for free); and the desired service
level (what percent of the time you must be or can afford to
be in stock) is the last factor. Mathematically these can be
combined to give a safety stock quantity to achieve the desired
service levels.

Not all inventory systems use these scientific safety stock
techniques. Distributors, especially small ones with unsophis-
ticated replenishment systems, and many retailers use rules
of thumb, like "Carry an extra month's forecasted sales," or
"Calculate the average demand over the lead time and add 50
percent."

The order-point technique applies principally to finished
goods management. Technicians call this independent demand; that is, customers buy what, when, and how much *they*
want. We, as vendors, have little control. In most cases,
customers don't even bother to read our forecasts!

The order-point technique contrasts sharply with the second
basic inventory management technique, material requirements
planning. This applies to dependent demand, demand that is
dependent on decisions we make. Items used to make finished
products have dependent demand. If the factory schedules a
batch of products to be completed in week 26 and the finishing
lead time is 2 weeks, then all components needed to make the
batch of finished goods must be available by week 24. This is
not a forecast; it is a simple calculation. Such calculations are
the basis of material requirements planning. The order-point
technique applies mainly to finished goods management;

material requirements planning applies to factory inventory management.

Material requirements planning is exemplified by the four-stage manufacturing process in Table 4-1. As part of the manufacturing process, some components are purchased and assembled with other components into a subassembly, the subassembly is combined with other components and subassemblies into a major assembly, and the major assembly is combined with other major assemblies to make the finished product. Only one chain is shown through the bill of material; that is, one purchased part is traced through one subassembly, one major assembly, and the finished product. However, all chains are linked together through this mechanism. I will use hard-goods terminology to describe the table. If you are more accustomed to "intermediates" instead of "subassemblies" or "major assemblies," and to "materials" or "ingredients" instead of "components" or "items," please forgive me. I am sure you will be able to make a successful translation.

The start is the master production schedule. This simply defines what the end-product delivery schedule should be. If the product is a make-to-stock item, then this schedule comes from the need to replenish the finished goods distribution system. A make-to-order item originates from a promise to deliver to the customer. The term "master" is used to denote the fact that this schedule controls the detailed schedules of all lower-level items. They are mathematically linked to the master.

In the example we plan to make three batches of finished product, one finishing in week 4, one in week 7, and the other in week 10. The batch quantities are 100 units. The lead time is 2 weeks, so we plan to start these through the finishing cycle in weeks 2, 5, and 8.

Our plan to start final production in weeks 2, 5, and 8 places dependent demand on all major assemblies in weeks 2, 5, and 8. The lead time to assemble our selected major assembly is 1 week. Its safety stock is zero. (That's called the gutsy approach!) The lot size or batch quantity will be "L4L," meaning "lot for lot." This means produce only for the real needs in a period, never more.

Table 4-1 Material Requirements Planning

	Week									
	1	2	3	4	5	6	7	8	9	10
Finished goods*										
Product complete				100			100			100
Planned start		100			100			100		
Major assembly†										
Dependent demand		100			100			100		
Free stock on hand	20	−80	−80	−80	−180	−180	−180	−280	−280	−280
Released factory orders										
New production needed		80			100			100		
Planned start	80			100			100			
Subassembly‡										
Dependent demand	80			100			100			
Free stock on hand	0	0	0	−100	−100	−100	−200	−200	−200	−200
Released factory orders	80									
New production needed				100			100			
Planned start		100			100					

Table 4-1   Material Requirements Planning (*Continued*)

	Week									
	1	**2**	**3**	**4**	**5**	**6**	**7**	**8**	**9**	**10**
Purchased item¶										
Dependent demand		100			100					
Free stock on hand	30	110	110	110	10	10	10	10	10	10
Released purchase orders		180								
New purchases needed										
Planned start										

* LT = 2.
† LT = 1, SS = 0, LS = L4L, OH = 20.
‡ LT = 2, SS = 0, LS = L4L, OH = 0.
¶ LT = 4, SS = 20, LS = 180, OH = 50.
Note: LT = lead time, SS = safety stock, LS = lot size, L4L = lot for lot, OH = on-hand quantity.

The line "free stock on hand" is a mathematical calculation of what will happen to the inventory. "Free stock" means that which is freely available to cover need; there are no prior claims on this material. We have 20 on hand at the moment. This stays constant until week 2, when we need 100. So the net need is 80 units. The next needs are 100 units in week 5 and another 100 in week 8. The table shows these shortages rising incrementally, the way MRP displays are usually printed. The calculated needs are also the batch sizes of the replenishment orders because of the lot size rule. New production of 80 units is needed in week 2 and 100 units in weeks 5 and 8. With a 1-week lead time, the planned start of this production is weeks 1, 4, and 7.

The same mathematical calculation occurs for the subassembly. Its dependent requirements come from our plans to start making 80 major assemblies in period 1, and 100 each in periods 4 and 7. The 80 subassemblies needed in period 1 are covered by an outstanding factory order to make 80 subassemblies that is scheduled to be completed in period 1. The 100 requirements in periods 4 and 7 are not covered by inventory or released factory schedules. So new production is needed in these periods. A 2-week lead time means we must start these planned orders in periods 2 and 5.

Dependent demand for the purchased item is 100 in weeks 2 and 5, coming from our plans to make subassemblies. There are 50 purchased items in stock. Twenty of these are set aside as safety stock or a contingency buffer. So the free stock available for planning is 30 units. The lead time is 4 weeks and the lot size 180.

The 100 needed in week 2 are covered partially by the 30 free stock, and the remainder are covered by a released purchase order with a scheduled delivery date of week 2. The purchase order quantity is 180 units, so at the end of week 2 there will be 110 units free stock. This is sufficient to cover the 100 needed in week 5 and still have 10 free stock left over. The actual on-hand quantity at that time will be the free stock plus the safety stock or 30 units.

As you can see, this is a very logical and straightforward technique to plan and schedule a factory and its vendors. Once the factory decides what products to make, in what quantity, and at what time to make them, all detailed schedules are simply derived from this top-level plan. There is no need to forecast demand for these items or use past historical usage as with the order-point technique. The demand can be simply calculated.

A combination of the two techniques is called a "time-phased order-point." (An example is shown in Table 4-2.) This technique applies to independent demand, just like the regular order-point technique. However the forecast, instead of being used to calculate a reorder point, is used to determine future requirements. These future requirements are netted against inventories and released factory orders. New planned production can be predicted to cover forecasted sales.

Referring again to Table 4-2, the forecast of sales is 33 units per week. The assembly lead time is 2 weeks, safety stock 33

Table 4-2 Time-Phased Order Point

	Week									
	1	2	3	4	5	6	7	8	9	10
Forecast sales	33	33	33	33	33	33	33	33	33	33
Free stock on hand	83	50	17	−16	−49	−82	−1-15	−148	−181	−214
Released factory orders										
New production needed				100			100			100
Planned start		100			100			100		

Note: Lead time = 2, safety stock = 33, lot size = 100, on-hand quantity = 149.

units, lot size 100, and on-hand inventory 149. Today's free stock, on-hand inventory minus safety stock, is 116. At the end of week 1, assuming actual sales of 33, it will be 83. It will continue to decline until week 4, when it will be −16. A replenishment order is obviously needed, so the lot size of 100 is planned for receipt in week 4. With a lead time of 2 weeks this means it must start in week 2. This batch quantity will last until week 7, when free stock goes negative to −15. Another order is planned. The same condition of negative free stock occurs in week 10, so an additional order is planned for receipt in that week.

The time-phased order point gives visibility of the future. The straight order point does not. The planned start and new production lines are close to the master production schedule for this product. I say close to because in real life there may be capacity conflicts or uneven loads on resources to be checked before it can be called a real master production schedule. The observant reader probably already realizes that this master production schedule is the same as the one used in Table 4-1.

So a company making products to stock has a time-phased order point to define when the warehouse needs replenishing. This technique is a major input to the master production schedule. The company uses material requirements planning to schedule the factory and vendors to support this master schedule.

The time-phased order point can also be used effectively at various levels in a distribution network. Consider a company with a central warehouse adjacent to the factory, three regional warehouses, and nine local warehouses. The local warehouses get their inventory from the regional warehouses, which in turn get their stocks from the central warehouse. The central warehouse is replenished by factory production.

The time-phased order point can be used by the local warehouses. In this case, the "new production needed" line of Table 4-2 becomes "next delivery needed." The lead time is the transportation time from the regional warehouse to the local. Hence the "planned start" becomes a schedule for trucks or railcars to leave the regional warehouse.

Similarly, a time-phased order point at the regional warehouse uses its own forecasted sales (assuming it delivers some products direct to customers) as well as the planned needs of its local warehouses to total its requirements. In this case we have a hybrid situation of independent and dependent demands. When these have been netted against inventory, the next needed deliveries can be calculated. The lead time in this case is the transportation time necessary to get from the central to the regional warehouses. Planned start refers to the schedule for trucks or railcars to leave the central warehouse.

A time-phased order at the central warehouse completes the logistics chain and results in a master production schedule for the factory. This linking of distribution centers through the time-phased order point technique is called "distribution requirements planning."

The two primary techniques of inventory replenishment—order point and material requirements planning—and their kindred techniques—time-phased order point and distribution requirements planning—all use the same inventory parameters: lot sizes, safety stocks, and lead times. Since we have already discussed lead times, how they are set, and how the lead-time syndrome works, we will now discuss the remaining two parameters.

Much has been written about the theory and science of establishing lot sizes and safety stocks, but in actual practice they are more often set by judgment. I don't want to dwell on why the theory is rarely applied. I simply want to make the point that these levels can be set mathematically or by judgment. And in all the systems with which I am familiar, any mathematical calculation can be overridden by human judgment. We'll tackle the mathematics first.

Lot Sizes

The first formula that concerned itself with lot sizes was published in 1915 and is called the square root economic order quantity (EOQ) formula. It balances the cost of placing a replenishment order with the cost of carrying the resultant inventory. The actual formula is

$$\text{EOQ} = \sqrt{\frac{2 \times \text{annual usage} \times \text{ordering costs}}{\text{unit cost} \times \text{annual inventory carrying rate}}}$$

I would like you to focus on the EOQ and the annual usage, really the only two variables in the equation. Let's suppose we used the EOQ to calculate the lot sizes for the time-phased order point of Table 4-2.

Sales increase 3 percent and the forecast is revised up 3 percent. The new EOQ will increase by the factor of $\sqrt{1.03}$ or, after rounding off, by two pieces.

Another mathematical approach to lot sizing is to set the batches equal to the average forecasted sales in a certain number of periods. This is called the "period order quantity" or "weeks-of-supply" technique. The number of weeks is often linked to the ABC or Pareto class for the item. (Pareto is the Italian who gave us the significant-few and trivial-many laws from which ABC analysis developed.)

The expensive and high-usage items should be ordered frequently; hence their weeks-of-supply policy is set low. Referring back to Table 4-2, a 3-week supply policy would amount to approximately 100 pieces. Less expensive and lower-usage items are ordered less often, so they would normally have a higher weeks-of-supply policy.

If the forecast is increased by 3 percent in our example, by using a 3-week supply policy, the new lot size will increase by 3 pieces. But what if the weeks of supply were longer, say 13 weeks. In this case the new lot size will increase by 13 pieces! This would place an immediate demand on the resources supporting this inventory, either from another warehouse or from the factory itself. It makes no difference to the results, as we shall see later.

Safety Stock

And now to that great subject, safety stock—the security blanket of production and inventory control. The theoretically correct mathematical system considers the variability of demand for an item, its lead time, its lot size, the average annual demand, and a required service level.

A safety-stock value is calculated on the above factors. There are a variety of formulas to calculate safety stocks on the basis of the specified service level method and dependent on the distribution of demands. None are shown here. Suffice it to say that the inputs I defined are used in most safety-stock calculations.

Let's say that the variability of demand for an item and the required service level are fixed and not affected by changes in the other factors. This is a fair assumption and is mostly true except when there are large swings in average demand. If the average increases, the variability normally decreases and vice versa. But it takes significant changes in the average to be pertinent.

It's also true that the safety stock stays the same for reasonable average demand changes provided the lot size also increases. The annual demand and lot size are used to calculate how many times the item is exposed to stock-outs. If the annual demand and lot size increase or decrease roughly proportionally, then the exposure rate will be the same. (You are only exposed to stock-out just before the next replenishment lot arrives. Hence the lot size of an item divided into its annual usage defines the exposure frequency.) As we saw earlier with the lot size mathematics, lot sizes increase when average demand increases. With the square root EOQ method it is not a linear increase, but this method is not used very often and, for relatively small changes in demand, the nonlinearity is not significant. So the only pertinent variable is lead time. I am sure you're beginning to see the correlation between lead-time changes and safety-stock fluctuations.

Another common mathematical approach to safety stock is to express it as a function of the average demand. Two weeks forecasted usage can be easily calculated and the resulting inventory set aside for contingency purposes.

Still another approach is to relate safety stock to the average demand over the lead time. I mentioned this earlier. A judgment call, such as 50 percent of the average demand over the lead time, is a simple and understandable safety-stock calculation. But now we are linking average demand, lead time, and safety stock together. This is how the safety stock was calculated in Table 4-2.

So what happens to safety stocks when we increase average demand 3 percent? With the theoretically correct safety-stock calculation, nothing happens. With 2 weeks forecasted usage as the technique it increases 2 pieces, and with 50 percent of the demand over the lead time it increases 1 piece.

Multistage Logistics Chain

The changes brought about by mathematically calculating lot sizes and safety stocks have been very small so far. But bear in mind I have ignored lead-time changes where safety stocks are concerned. I hope you can feel that express train coming toward you. And I have also ignored human judgment, better defined as emotion, especially where inventories are concerned.

But even leaving aside lead-time changes and emotion, could small changes at one end of the logistics chain cause large changes at the other? You betcha!

Let's look at a five-stage distribution chain as shown in Figure 4-2. Vendors deliver material to a factory. The factory

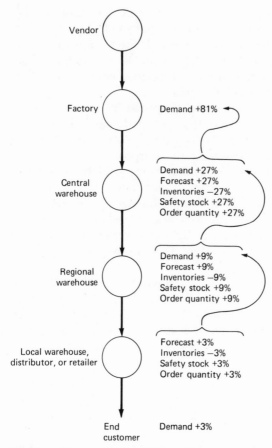

Fig. 4-2 Five-stage distribution channel.

produces products and sends them to the central warehouse. The central warehouse supports the regional warehouses, which in turn support the local warehouses. Customers buy from the local warehouses only. (This is an unlikely scenario in the real world since the regional and central warehouses probably would serve some customers directly. This confuses my message so I have omitted this complication. This complicating factor also confuses the people managing these warehouses concerning what is really happening, so in this sense it also aggravates the real situation.) In the real world there are obviously many vendors supplying the factory, the central warehouse supplies several regional warehouses, and each regional warehouse supplies several local warehouses or distributors. Only one chain has been shown for clarity.

The warehouses use order points, time-phased or not, to tell them when to replenish inventory. Both forms of the order point react the same way to demand changes, so it makes no difference to the result. The plant uses a master production schedule and material requirements planning for factory and vendor scheduling.

The simpler mathematical techniques for lot sizing and safety stock are used by all distribution points. Lot sizes are calculated by using a predetermined number of weeks of supply, and safety stocks are set at 50 percent of the average demand expected during the replenishment lead time. The lead times are all 2 weeks. This simple example will show clearly what is happening. Aggregate customer demand increases 3 percent at the local warehouses. The forecasted sales are increased by this amount for the future. With higher sales, inventories at the local warehouses drop 3 percent. Safety stocks and order quantities increase 3 percent.

The cumulative effect of all these small changes is a 9 percent increase in short-term demand at the regional warehouses. (The inventory dropped 3 percent, the safety stock increased 3 percent, and the order quantity increased 3 percent.) The regional warehouses see this increased demand and update their forecast of sales by 9 percent. They now go through a similar calculation routine for lot sizes and safety stocks and send a 27 percent higher short-term demand to the central warehouse. The central warehouse mathematics magnifies this to an 81 percent short-term change in demand on the factory. Presto, one joker! Now we're off and running. And of course the reverse is true. A 3 percent reduction in customer demand can be shown to create an 81 percent short-term reduction in factory schedules.

Does this distortion happen in the real world? Obviously not as clearly as shown in the example, but it does happen. Ask the factories that make products for stock, ''Are your demands stable or highly variable?'' The almost universal answer is, "Highly variable, and from no real cause that we can identify." The main cause is due to inventory policies in their replenishment systems. They magnify small changes at the customer demand end of the logistics chain into large variations at the supply end.

With today's extensive use of computers the fluctuation of perceived demand is even more scary. Can you imagine the inventories in the above example being planned and scheduled by computer? Mathematics built into the computer programs automatically adjusts forecasts, safety stocks, and lot sizes. Some programs even print the replenishment orders automatically. All that remains is mailing them out. Other programs even eliminate that step and communicate directly with the computer at the supply station, so the entire process is untouched by human hand!

But what happens at the factory and with the vendor? The factory just received an 81 percent increase in short-term demand. One of two things normally happens. If the factory is well managed, they realize their capacity cannot handle this increase in the short term. Hence they carefully plan how to phase in the extra capacity over a period of time. The central warehouse orders now needed to replenish their low stocks cannot be supplied. So the factory extends the lead time for these products.

Mathematics comes rushing to the rescue! At the central warehouse, the lead-time increase is factored into the safety-stock equation, and the planned safety stocks automatically increase. This increase reduces the free stocks even further, so additional replenishment orders are released to the factory. Even longer lead times are the inevitable result.

The central warehouse is low on stocks because they have all been shipped to the regional warehouses. When the next regional warehouse demand occurs, it is possible that the central warehouse cannot meet the demand. The regional warehouse is quoted the factory lead time for the next delivery. They adjust the lead times in their system, increase the planned safety stocks, and place even more orders with the central warehouse. This is seen as incremental demand. Forecasts, lot sizes, and safety stocks are again increased against a larger out-of-stock condition. More demands are placed on the factory.

The chain is broken when the factory's capacity is significantly increased. Products start flowing into the distribution chain, lead times start dropping, but now the mathematics creates an overreaction. Forecasts, safety stocks, and lot sizes are all reduced at a time when the inventory is high. A shutoff of orders to the factory is the result. The vendor goes through an even greater boom-and-bust cycle because of the factory's inventory system, as we shall see later.

An alternative scenario occurs when the factory is poorly managed. Managers quickly change their master production schedule to reflect the 81 percent demand increase. But it is a rare company that can successfully handle a short-term increase in demand of 81 percent. And it's even rarer still to find a company where all its vendors can adjust to such an increase.

But the master production schedule is changed. The mathematics of material requirements planning converts this master production schedule into detailed schedules for the plant and into purchase orders for the vendors. Presto, jokers for the vendors! Some vendors deliver the extra material, either because they have it in stock (the vendor could be a local warehouse for industrial products) or because their capacities are flexible. But some vendors will not deliver. They simply extend lead times.

In the factory, demands are 81 percent higher on each work center, straining the available resources. Again, some work centers will be able to handle this extra demand and produce the needed items; others will not. The only choice they have is to extend the lead times on items *they* produce.

Is it clear what extending lead times in a factory does? Refer to Table 4-2 again. If the lead time of the major assembly is increased to 2 weeks, the new production-needed date doesn't change. The planned start date changes to 1 week earlier. This cascades through the subassemblies and onto all purchased items. Here come even more jokers. And more important still, the 81 percent factory demand is increased even more for the vendors. The factory's inventory system also amplifies demand on its suppliers. The end result of this scenario is shortages and excesses at the same time. The vendors who don't deliver on time create shortages, and those that do create excesses— excesses because the capacity of the plant is inadequate to process these inventories or because other parts needed to match up with the excesses are short. A similar process occurs with the resources inside the factory. The total inventories grow because the inflow into the plant exceeds the outflow.

And now we come to the worst problem of all. Some people call it human judgment, but it should be called emotion.

Emotion

Where inventories are concerned, the pressure is always for more. Inventory systems are organized to tell us when inventories are low and need replenishing. This is a constant activity. Evaluating when inventories are in excess is not done routinely. It is only done when the total inventory levels attract top management's eye and they demand inventories be reduced. This emphasis on shortages only is especially true of inventory management in a factory.

Shortages are the main point of discussion in a plant or warehouse. Some companies even have meetings once a day to discuss them. These meetings are variously called shortage meetings, confrontations, negative availability meetings, the lie club, or in one company I know of, morning prayers! "Is that part here yet?" "I don't know, boss, but I'm praying it's on the receiving dock." The emphasis is on getting more, obviously to solve the shortages.

Our dealings with vendors are always for more. We rate vendors on their delivery performance either mathematically or subjectively. Well, that's not quite true. We rate them on their failure to deliver *early enough*. In other words, late deliveries are bad but early deliveries in most plants pass unnoticed. Don't forget the biased penalty rating of the lead-time syndrome game and what it caused.

To prove this, go ask your inventory or purchasing people, "How well does our system identify late or early deliveries from vendors?" My guess is it identifies late deliveries well, early deliveries poorly. Then ask them, "How effectively do we react to late and early deliveries?" My guess is that late deliveries are reacted to well by expediting them, while early deliveries, if they are detected, are accepted unless there is unusual pressure for inventory reduction, such as at the end of the fiscal year. On a consistent basis, though, knowledge and action occur on late deliveries and probably not on early deliveries.

The sales departments of the world say they are concerned about customer service, but in actual fact they are really concerned about customer *disservice*. Their interest is in those inventories that are too low. They could care less about the excesses. So the pressure is again for more. As we all know, because our sales departments never tire of telling us, "You can't sell from an empty wagon." (Unless you're selling empty wagons themselves, of course.)

The pressure for more to cover shortages triggers emotional responses that are 180 degrees out of phase with what should be done. Not only do the shortages get worse, but the demand for products is magnified throughout the logistics chain, as in the warehouses example cited earlier.

Inventory planners, after being hit with so many shortages that their production is affected, will increase planned safety stocks for their parts. Increasing planned safety stocks does not mean that the actual stocks increase; it means more stock is set aside as safety, reducing the free stocks. More orders are placed on the resources supplying these parts to build the added safety margins. Increasing *actual* stocks takes capacity and time.

When purchasing people have vendors who are behind schedule or when they are quoted longer lead times, they release orders even earlier than the inflated lead times require and they order more than they need. Again demands on the vendor resources increase.

Salespeople use a number of tricks to get more. They turn in overly optimistic sales forecasts to fool the factory into overproducing. They tell their good customers any time they hear the factory is getting busy, "Get your orders in earlier to save your place in the queue. And order a little extra, just to be on the safe side." (I am sure you cannot see an ulterior motive here.) They demand more safety stocks on their finished goods inventories, especially when customer service starts to drop. Demands are increased again.

But the major reason for shortages, late vendors, and poor customer service is demand that exceeds supply. Planning more inventory and therefore increasing the demands even more is not the solution. It's exactly the wrong approach. Even if the reason for shortages is not related to demand exceeding supply but is more a function of making the wrong things, safety stocks again cannot help. When priorities on jobs are wrong or are being ignored, the wrong parts get made and excesses and shortages result simultaneously. Safety stocks planned into an inventory management system simply distort the priorities by asking for parts earlier than needed. They cause more incorrect priorities. They do not ensure getting the right parts at the right time but instead plan the opposite.

And of course safety-stock theory only applies to a certain set of conditions. Demand must be random, preferably evenly distributed around the average, not skewed, and observed often enough that statistical analysis can apply. These conditions pertain to most items in the distribution world.

But what about manufacturing? Here, none of these conditions apply. The demand is dependent and in most cases infrequent because of lot sizing. Can you imagine thinking you can predict the triple-forecast error when lead times are long, say over 20 weeks, in the dependent world? It's ridiculous! But believe it or not, that's what inventory planners, schedulers, and purchasing people do on a regular basis. They order more sooner and increase planned safety stocks of their parts. And this is called judgment?

We have some recent experiences that are classic in showing this emotional "more" phenomenon. The Arab oil embargo of 1973 caused gasoline demand to exceed supply very slightly. The reaction of everyone was to buy more. Gas tanks, instead of being allowed to go to one-quarter full before being refilled, were refilled at three-quarters full. As a result, the average gas tank in every car and truck was carrying another one-quarter tank. Thus hundreds of millions of gallons of fuel were unused at any given time. (This figure does not include all the gasoline stored in garages in gasoline cans and other containers.) To make matters even worse, the extra weight being carried in all these vehicles caused gasoline mileage to drop, and as a result, demand increased even more over supply.

Johnny Carson on the *Tonight* show once said, "Ladies and gentlemen, did you know there is going to be a toilet paper shortage?" That's all he said. Several days later, toilet paper was as scarce as hen's teeth. I've still got some stockpiled!

One day when visiting a plant, I got an urgent request to visit the boardroom. On my way there I wondered what I had done wrong or whose feet I had stepped on. The vice presidents of sales, manufacturing, and finance and the general manager were in the boardroom. I said, "Hi, folks, what's up?" The vice president of sales set me straight quickly with "Nothing's up. It's all down, especially customer service." I said, "Oh, how good is it?" She said, "No, how bad is it?" "OK," I said, "have it your way. How bad is it?" (The company I was visiting makes products to stock. They measure customer service by the percent of line items on customers' orders that they ship complete within 24 hours after receipt of the order.) The vice president of sales said, "It's 43 percent and dropping. I have spoken to a very qualified planner in inventory control who has just passed the inventory management examination, and he told me if we had another $500,000 in finished goods inventory, the service level would go up to about 95 percent, which is the service policy of our company. The vice president of finance has told me that the increased sales this will generate, coupled with faster receivables and less paperwork and confusion in the factory, will give a 30 percent return on this investment. This meeting is to approve the addition of $500,000 in safety stock spread over all our items to get the service from 43 percent to 95 percent."

You have to admit, the vice president of sales had done her homework. Instead of complaining about the service level, she had someone calculate the additional assets needed to improve it and someone else figure out the return on these assets.

There was only one question she did not ask: Is the capacity of the factory adequate to support ongoing sales and build the additional $500,000 of inventory? The answer was no! The reason for the poor customer service was that demand was 30 percent above forecast but the factory had only managed to raise capacity by 20 percent. They were aggressively trying to add more capacity, but they had exhausted all the quick methods, like overtime and subcontracting, to get the increase of 20 percent. To go beyond this meant hiring skilled people, initiating multiple shifts, and buying some new equipment, and these all take time and money. Demand increases can be almost instantaneous, especially with our wonderful computerized inventory systems, but supply increases always take longer.

What would have happened if this group had agreed to the request for more inventory? Planned safety stocks of all their finished goods items would have been increased, reducing the free stocks and triggering even more demands on an already overloaded factory. The people in the factory would have been forced to make choices. They would have made what was needed plus safety stock of some parts, but nothing of others. The service level would then have dropped even more as stock-out items increased even though there would have been plenty of stock of some parts on hand.

They were lucky in this case to be talking about the total impact of safety stocks on their system. The capacity implications were clear to see. But in the majority of cases safety stock is not planned in this manner. People at various levels of the organization make isolated decisions concerning their products and parts, and the total effect is not seen. But the total effect is there; an overloading of already overloaded facilities. More shortages result causing more isolated decisions, and the problem just gets worse.

My recommendation to the vice president of sales was to reduce the planned safety stocks instead of increasing them. This would temporarily close the gap between demand and supply because the stored capacity in inventory would assist in meeting demands. I finally persuaded her to reduce all planned safety stocks to zero to let the factory work on the real customer demand and inventory needs. As we left the boardroom, she asked, "May I hire you? I went into that room convinced I needed more safety stock and here I am, not entirely convinced, but persuaded I need less. And that less safety stock in the plan will increase customer service. If you can sell me on that, you can sell anybody anything!" I politely refused, but called her several weeks later to ask, "How's your customer service level today?" She replied, "It's at 75 percent and still going up. If I hadn't seen it for myself, I would never have believed it!"

The increased customer service level was obviously only a temporary condition. As soon as the pool of inventory set aside as safety stock had been drained, the imbalance of demand over supply took the service level back down again. All that reducing safety stocks did was to give the factory more time to expand capacity to meet the demand.

The real tragedy in this story is that a large part of the increased demand was a result of inventory variables changing at a higher level of the logistics chain. Much of the capacity that was eventually added was not needed for the real demand but only for increasing their customers' inventories. As soon as the cycle broke, as it always does, excess idle capacity and large layoffs occurred. The company under discussion suffered several years before recovering enough business to become profitable again.

It may be tough to admit, but I hope I have persuaded you that increased sales are often externally caused. They are not the result of better advertising, sales campaigns, design, or quality; rather, they are the result of someone at a higher level in the supply chain changing the inventory parameters.

We usually blame external factors when sales drop but rarely when they increase. The recession, high interest rates, and dumping by foreign competition are thought to be the causes when sales drop, but we get carried away with high opinions of our performance when sales increase. The demand changes in both cases are largely externally influenced, not internally.

The terrible danger of this biased psychology is that when business booms, we are led to believe the boom will continue forever. But demands that come from planned inventory increases are false, the worst kind, because at some point the bust cycle will be needed to return them to more normal levels.

Reverse Inventory Management

The theory and management of inventory is highly questionable. I said earlier that it is exactly wrong. Combine this fact with the emotional reactions of people concerned with inventories and you have the seeds of disaster happily in place in every inventory situation. They are there just waiting for the initial shock to start them growing and flourishing, building wrong inventories and more inventories when the opposite should occur.

This pressure for more inventory will be a recurring theme throughout the book. Where's the pressure for less? The answer: It will come only when management issues an edict, "There will be less!" Such an edict will put emotion on the back burner. The insistence of the boss and the threat of losing your job will put more attention on inventory reduction, and inventories will come down. But now supply will exceed demand and, while we live off the inventory, our factories will be shut down, our vendors will suffer from a lack of orders, layoffs and unemployment will rise, and machines and factories will operate way below capacity. Don't worry, though; this situation won't last long. The pressure for more is still very much alive and well. All we need is one more shortage and. . . .

It's true, though, that inventory management *is* exactly wrong. A primary function of stocks should be to act as a dampener between demand and supply variations. If demand picks up, inventories should reduce until supplies can react, and vice versa. But the reverse is built into our inventory calculations and emotional psyche. When demand picks up, forecasts, lot sizes, and safety stocks all go up. Demand is amplified, not dampened. When capacity constraints force lead times to lengthen, logical mathematics causes chaos. When shortages occur or the grapevine warns of capacity problems, emotion overrides even the inflated mathematics, and as a result, more is ordered sooner.

This process is an interesting phenomenon. When the economy is good, consumer confidence is high, so everyone buys. But when business confidence is low, not about the economy but about being able to get needed products on time to support the economy, safety stocks are increased, more is ordered, inventories grow, shortages grow, and business loses even more confidence about supporting the economy.

When interest rates rise because of the demand from businesses to finance their extra inventories, management turns their attention to the total stock levels. Safety stocks and lot sizes are reduced, and as a result the demands on factories are reduced. Suddenly supply exceeds demand, lead times start falling and layoffs occur. Consumers start to lose their confidence just as business confidence increases. Buying stops, dropping lead times even more. Since lead time is a factor in calculating safety stocks, these planned stocks are reduced again as lead times reduce. Even less demand is passed upstream, and as a result lead times reduce again. And round and round we go. Inventories now cause the slightly lesser demand to become a huge reduction in demands on factories, especially those at the bottom of the supply chain, like primary metal producers.

This ability of inventories to disturb the true relationship between supply and demand is a major contributor to boom-and-bust cycles. The combination of current inventory theory, systems, and emotion transforms small changes in demand into huge changes in supply. The three factors of lead time, safety stock, and lot sizes feed on each other and are powerful modifiers of the supply-and-demand relationship. But that wonderful human trait, emotion, is the worst factor of all.

Chapter Five

Disturbed Flow Rates

So far we have discussed the theory of how inventory variables and lead times affect the economy. If you would like some real-life examples to prove that theory works in practice, refer to Chapter 11. I hope, however, that you have related enough of your own past problems to the theory for you to know that these are real effects.

But the picture is not yet complete. There's even more bad news on the way. Let's look a little deeper at the problem and see what else we can uncover.

Inventory is always assumed to be good. It is carried on the books as current assets, the same as cash. It is assumed to have quick convertibility into money. But in reality inventory can be a lot stickier than money. Only if it's the right stuff is it quickly convertible to cash. If it's the wrong stuff, it is neither quick to convert nor convertible to full value on the books.

How about your inventory? How much is the wrong stuff? Annual obsolescence charges are some indication, but the real problem is often hidden as good materials. You don't want to take the write-off this year and hurt the bottom line. What about the excess materials? It doesn't matter how you define excess, although more than a year's supply would probably be a good definition. How much excess does your company have? Many companies don't even know. They have poor, nonexistent, or unenforced procedures to identify excess materials. But these excess materials are a drain on the business, almost as bad as obsolete inventories, given today's interest rates.

How do you get obsolete or excess materials? As Evert Welch, formerly director of production and inventory control for ITT in New York, said, "You have obsolete inventory because you bought or made too much of that item the last time." Sound right to you? Of course it's right. The question is, "Why did it happen? What caused someone to buy or make too much of the item?"

I mentioned in Chapter 2 that every order placed is three forecasts. Inventory is only created when someone orders it. Let's explore this idea further.

Every order, whether to buy something or make something, defines an item, a quantity, and a date. But when I say "defines," I really mean "forecasts." An order is placed at the start of the lead time, so the order definition relates to a future need. Statisticians tell us that forecast accuracy worsens the further into the future you try to forecast, as represented by the trumpet shape of Figure 2-16. So the three forecasts that all orders represent are highly influenced by our old friend lead time. The longer the lead time is, the more inaccurate all three forecasts will be.

The quality of products flowing is therefore a concern. When I mention quality, I'm not referring to how well a product performs; I'm asking, "Is what we're producing the right stuff?" If it's the wrong stuff, our problem is much worse than we have thought so far.

Disturbed Operational Flow Rates

Products flowing through our logistics chains can be categorized into three groupings.

Required: The required flow rate is the amount of goods needed to flow from supplier to user to support the user's production or sales needs. The required rate of flow is linked to the internal manufacturing plans of the user or to the

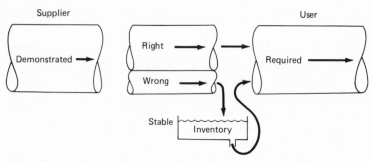

Fig. 5-1 Product flows.

expected sales of the distributor. It is a future rate that can be calculated mathematically by using our logistics systems.

Demonstrated: The demonstrated flow rate is the amount of goods actually flowing, an average of the short-term past. The demonstrated rate of flow should match the required rate of flow; it should be neither larger nor smaller. If it is larger, we build inventory; if it is smaller, we create shortages.

Effective: The effective flow rate is that portion of the demonstrated flow rate that is the right quantity of the right items at the right time. By definition, effective flow rates are always smaller than demonstrated flow rates because of hedging for a strike, planning for a vacation shutdown, producing in economical lots, or handling a seasonal sales pattern. The question is, "How low is the effective flow rate at a point in time compared with the demonstrated flow rate?"

Figure 5-1 shows the relation between these flow rates conceptually. A supplier's production or shipments, his or her demonstrated capacity, can be broken into two segments. One is the right amount of the right things at the right time, and the other is those things that are wrong in at least one way—the wrong things, the wrong amounts, or the wrong times. The right materials obviously go to the user's facility to support production or sales. The wrong things end up in inventory, either at the supplier's plant or at the user's.

If the wrong things are not too wrong—that is, if the triple-forecast error problem is small—the wrong things will sit in inventory for a while and then become the right things. These can then be withdrawn from stock to support the user's needs in combination with the right things. In such a situation the inventory of wrong things remains constant. New wrong things flow in at the same rate as wrong things become right and flow out.

What happens if the supplier makes a larger share of wrong things, for example, when lead times lengthen or the inventory variables change? Obviously, the inventories of wrong things grow as more wrong things flow in than flow out. The amount of right things the user gets is less than what is needed, so the user experiences shortages. You know that shortages are a heinous crime for inventory planners and schedulers; when threatened with shortages, they release more orders to suppliers. The suppliers see this as increased demand and expand their demonstrated flow rates. This process is illustrated in Figure 5-2. When suppliers increase their demonstrated flow rates, enough right things are received by the user. But there is a penalty: growing inventories of the wrong things. At some point, the costs of financing these inventories become too high

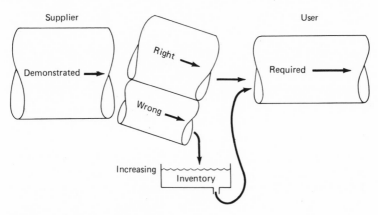

Fig. 5-2 Inflated product flows.

and an edict is given to cut them. A reduction in inventories is achieved either by returning them to the supplier, or by forcing emotion onto the back burner so that planned safety stocks are cut and lot sizes reduced.

When these things are accomplished, the demonstrated flow rate of the supplier must drop below the required flow rate of the user. Of course a more painful way of dropping inventories is by writing them off because they are obsolete. And *you* know what that costs a business. The company with the wrong inventory, user or supplier, gets hurt most by this obsolescence. The majority of obsolete inventory comes from the scenario just described, and not from technological change.

The primary factor causing effective flow rates to be below demonstrated ones is lead times. Keeping in mind the triple-forecast error problem and the fact that forecasts are more wrong the further out they are made, it follows that long lead times and effective flow rates are diametrically opposed.

During periods of inventory growth and lead-time escalation, most businesses feel they have inadequate capacity. But shipments (demonstrated flow rates) are higher than consumption (required capacity). At the same time shortages of items reach record levels. How can this be? Effective flow rates are the problem. Lead times up to 60 weeks are not uncommon for bearings, castings, forgings, semiconductors, and many other commodity groups. Calculating that far in advance, you tell me how well you can predict what customers will buy or what your factory will need. Factories are then directed to make more than is needed and are pressured for more to fill the shortages. As a result, inventories grow filled with things that are not required, and capacity is added. You now see the role the die plays in the lead-time syndrome demonstration.

The Real Lead-Time Problem

So far we have talked about lead times designated for making or buying an item. But that is not the extent of the lead-time

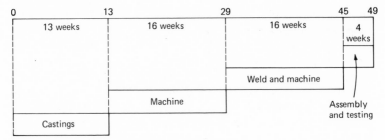

Fig. 5-3 Stacked lead-time example.

problem. It's much worse. Figure 5-3 shows the buildup of lead times to make a product. This is variously called the critical path lead time, stacked lead time, or manufacturing and procurement cycle time. We have to predict what products our customer will buy at the end of this product trajectory. Calculations can then be made of what detailed factory and vendor schedules (part numbers, quantities, and dates) will be needed to support this prediction.

I drew this picture while talking to a machining supervisor. He was complaining about the poor performance of the purchasing group. Specifically his complaint was, "They are buying all the wrong castings." I asked him, "Do you mean they aren't buying enough castings?" He said, "No, we have a yard full of castings. We're up to you-know-where with castings. But they're all the wrong ones!"

The lead time for castings was 13 weeks. But this wasn't the problem. Castings aren't bought just for themselves. They're bought to make something that, it is hoped, a customer will buy after it is completed. In this case the stacked lead time was 49 weeks. How good is your forecast that far out? Remember the trumpet shape of Figure 2-16! And if the forecast is *not* good, what is purchasing buying today? The answer: all the wrong things. How else can a factory have a yard full of castings yet blame purchasing for poor performance? Is there any question that effective capacity was low?

How does this picture relate to the total economy? The stacked lead time from the creation of raw materials until the purchasing of an end item by a consumer, when you consider all tiers of supply, is enormous. It also fluctuates greatly, depending on whether it occurs in the boom or in the bust phase of the economic cycle. You can now see how the boom feeds on itself, more wrong forecasts triggering more unnecessary production, until the inevitable collapse.

In the case of the machining supervisor, we quickly analyzed what the required rate of casting deliveries should have been to make the volume of products the customers needed. We then went back to the receiving documents and calculated how much had been received recently on the average, in other words the demonstrated capacity. It was about 5 percent above the required rate. You knew that before I told you, didn't you? How else can you build inventory? But the tragedy, as it always is, is that the inventory was the wrong stuff. Ineffective flow rates strike again.

Another misconception is that inventories reduce the stacked lead time. Instead they do just the opposite. There is no question that inventories, assuming they are the right things, can reduce the lead time a customer is given. But when we talk about stacked lead time, forecast accuracy, and effective flow rates, especially at the procurement point, stocks only serve to lengthen the process.

For example, look at how stock changes the pattern of Figure 5-3 into that of Figure 5-4. Assume we carry an average of a 2-month stock of rough castings plus a 2-month stock of finished goods. We have just succeeded in pushing the average time between a customer purchase and the date a purchase order is placed from 49 to 65 weeks. Have we made progress or made matters worse?

One of my clients has several factories that produce in a chain. The first produces the basic raw materials, and these flow through the other factories, being processed into higher and higher levels of completion until the last factory makes the customer end-products. There are several stages of distribution after this, which extend the chain even more. These distribution levels can be conceived as further levels of production, getting the product closer to the end customer.

When he charted all the factory lead times and the average time raw materials, semifinished products, and the finished goods stayed in stock, he found the stacked lead time between procurement of raw materials and customer purchase was 24 months. Two years for a product that retails for less than one dollar! Can you imagine a business in which you buy materials today and wait 24 months for this to be converted back into cash? The risk alone, not even including the business costs, should scare you to death. Can you imagine asking an investor to commit money for an investment that won't pay out for 24 months? The estimated payout is pretty good, but there is a significant risk the payout will be zero, or much later than the 24-month estimate. I doubt you'll get many investors lining

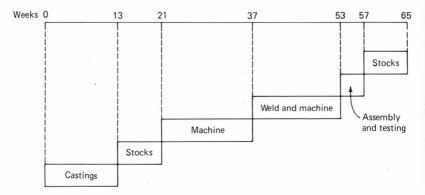

Fig. 5-4 Stacked lead time with stocks.

up for your offer. But isn't that what a manufacturer or distributor does on a regular schedule? It may not be to the same degree as in this example, but nonetheless the same concepts apply.

Now how about worldwide purchasing? What about that new plant we are building in Singapore? And there are some really good prices in Korea. We have to shop around and use worldwide purchasing practices in today's economy.

It is easy enough to make trade-offs between the cost savings and the extra transportation stocks we need when we manufacture or buy overseas or at great distances. It is a straightforward return on investment calculation, muddied of course by exchange rates, preferential tax treatment, and the like. But these variables can be reasonably defined. What is difficult to include in the trade-offs is diminished flexibility to change, a higher level of slow-moving and obsolete stocks, and disruption at the user plant because of shortages. These are all real costs but hard to find in the financial chart of accounts. So we continue to separate suppliers and manufacturers on the basis of financial analysis, considering only half the variables. We set up separate stocking and manufacturing points in a product's manufacturing cycle and make an item retailing for less than one dollar with a stacked lead time of 24 months. And then we wonder about the annual obsolescence charges, manufacturing variances, and customer complaints about inflexibility.

The use of the sales price of an item to question the accepted lead times is a very simple way of focusing attention on the lead-time problem. I was discussing lead times for electric motors with a purchasing agent one day. I asked him, "How long are they?" He said, "8 weeks." My next question was, "How much do you pay for these motors on average?" He said, "$100." Now we can calculate the number of standard hours needed to produce a motor by estimating the factory costs, probably around $60, estimating the burdened labor portion, probably around $25, and dividing by a labor rate of $12.50 per hour; it comes out nicely to 2 hours. And the lead time for a motor is 8 weeks!

I have had similar discussions on the lead times for castings, which were 13 weeks when the labor content was estimated at no more than 30 minutes; machinists files, where the lead times were 6 months with a labor content of 5 minutes; bearings, where the lead times were 12 months with a labor content of 1 hour, and so on. In all cases the labor content was a ridiculously small part of the quoted lead time. Now I realize you make some parts in batches, which increases the time, and sometimes there are special materials to be purchased, and this is part of the lead time, but even so the disparity is enormous. The lead time is certainly not related to the real-world actions necessary to produce the product.

We prove this every time we are given a very urgent product to make, maybe at the general manager's insistence. Things that normally take 6 weeks to make are made on the night shift and shipped the next day. How could this be possible if the real lead time was 6 weeks? It couldn't be. But luckily for the general managers and their customers, real lead times are always a minute portion of those quoted. This allows us to regularly "pull these rabbits out of the hat," of course, always at the expense of other jobs that now have a longer lead time.

Inventory Flow in the Manufacturing World

Inventories are an element in many businesses, for example, retailers, restaurants, distributors, and manufacturers. Some businesses manage them better than others, especially most retailers and restaurants, while others are beset by the problems described in the previous chapters.

I would like to focus your attention on one business segment—manufacturing—to make the problem clearer and get us closer to the solution. But even this subject is too broad because some manufacturers, especially some segments of the process industry, manage inventories well. This is not because they have realized the problem of inventory management, but because they have no choice. Either their volume is too great to store or so relatively small, that controlled inventories are mandatory, or short shelf life means the product must be used quickly or it deteriorates. Milk is a good example of the latter instance.

Let's reduce the scope even further to fabrication and assembly businesses, which employ most workers in manufacturing. Clothing, furniture, and appliances are examples of consumer products, while valves, pumps, switches, relays, and business equipment are examples of industrial products, all made by the fabrication and assembly industry.

The fabrication and assembly industry is made up of a few

large plants and very many small- to medium-size factories. And it's also important to recognize that, with few exceptions, these plants function as autonomous entities even though many are part of large corporations. Planning, scheduling, and the management of inventories is delegated to each plant's management. Again I trust that the distributors and retailers reading this book are not offended by my focus on manufacturing. You will see many parallels to your operations by studying the manufacturing environment. It is also important to realize that many distributors and retailers handle products made by the fabrication and assembly industry. There are many inventory stocking points along the road from producing raw materials to getting these finished products in the hands of the end consumer. So the impact of this industrial segment on the supply chain must be kept in mind. It's a critical segment. But for now, let's just look at one manufacturing plant.

A Microcosm

First let's define the environment. The plant is a fabricator and assembler of reasonably complex products; it's not important what the products are. They buy 10,000 different raw materials, parts, and assemblies, and manufacture an equivalent number themselves. In all, 20,000 items are managed by their inventory system. They sell 200 standard products but also assemble an almost infinite range of variations from these standard units made to customer's order. This is a fair picture of the typical hard-goods manufacturer.

What do you think is emphasized by the inventory planners and schedulers in this factory? It's obvious isn't it? With 20,000 things to manage, having enough of all the right things at the right time is crucial. Hence their attention is focused on managing all these specific items, one at a time. Earlier I said inventory management was a micro process, and here is an example in operation.

The inventory management system, MRP, as described in Chapter 4, supports this emphasis on specifics. It provides messages to the pertinent inventory planners, schedulers, and buyers of which items need replenishing when. It also tells when already released orders for replenishment of specific items are incorrectly scheduled, for delivery either too early or too late. Nowhere are these exceptions added together so management can see their total impact.

We also know the bias of inventory management is to more. Shortages are the heinous crime, so attention is placed on releasing new orders and expediting late ones. Slowing down the early orders gets little or no attention unless a top management edict forces a reduction in stocks.

This attention to specifics permeates the whole organization. Salespeople are interested in the specific promised delivery date given to a specific customer order. Purchasing people communicate information about specific needed deliveries to their vendors. Schedulers concentrate on the next specific jobs to be run on specific machines. Even top managers get involved with specific customer deliveries, especially when the deliveries are late!

But the sum of many specific decisions is a required rate of flow, either from the factory to its customers, from vendors into the factory, or through the various factory resources.

Rates of flow, however, are rarely considered and even less often measured. If you don't believe me, ask a supervisor, especially a fabrication supervisor, this question: "Last week, did those machines you manage produce at the rate of flow needed to execute our production schedule?" It's a rare supervisor who can give you a quantitative answer to this question. Instead you will probably be told which items are on the "hot" list and which items are currently in production, a specifics answer to a flow-rate question.

As another test, ask the buyer responsible for your worst vendor, "Did that vendor deliver enough product across our receiving dock to execute our production schedule last week?" (A flow-rate question.) You will rarely get a quantitative answer to this question. Instead you will hear, "The vendor is late on all these items," another specifics answer to a flow-rate question.

Is information about specifics (shortages, late deliveries, and hot lists) a clear measure of a flow-rate problem (capacity shortfall or bottleneck)? Or could there be two diseases, with shortages the symptom of either one?

A vendor with inadequate capacity to serve all his or her customers will create shortages at most of them. A vendor with adequate capacity but working on the right things at the wrong time will also cause customers to have shortages. The symptom is the same. It's the solutions that are different. Expediting in the first case will be fruitless. Additional capacity in this vendor's plant or using another vendor with available capacity is the only solution. But expediting could pay off in the second case.

We fail too many times to define the disease before we attack the symptoms. We take aspirin to cure a headache caused by banging our heads against a brick wall. The number of specific items in the inventory system focuses our attention on the symptom—shortages—not on the disease. And hence the solution often escapes us.

Consider a typical discussion between a buyer and the salesperson from her worst vendor, worst because of late deliveries, hence shortages. The meeting starts out with handshakes and the normal small talk about the weather or the salesperson's trip. Then they get down to business.

The buyer is primed for action. On her desk is a pile of late orders the vendor has not delivered. She starts out with the top one.

Buyer: How come this order is 3 months past due? We ordered this item with your quoted lead time, but here it is late. When will we get it?

Salesperson: The factory is working on it right now. It should be shipped this week. We're sorry if we hurt your production. But just to set the record straight (and now the salesperson digs into *his* briefcase and pulls out *his* pile of orders), you see this order here? We normally quote a 6-

week lead time but you needed some urgently. We produced in 2 weeks and got you out of trouble.

Buyer: Oh! Well. Let's see. This next order here, you're over
2 months late on this item. What's the latest delivery date
on this order?

Salesperson: That order is in fabrication right now. We had
some real trouble with the tooling. The factory gave us a
shipping promise of 2 weeks from now.

But, do you see this order? (He then takes the next one
off *his* pile.) It was a new part your engineers wanted
made quickly. We didn't even have tooling so we had to
use our most skilled people (yes, you guessed it, the tool-
room people) to make it. We delivered it just 1 week after
receiving the specs. I call that good service, don't you?

Buyer: Oh! Well. See this order here, you're. . . .

And on and on it goes, with both parties getting more and
more frustrated as they discuss specifics. But specifics are
dynamic, so you should expect some things to be needed
earlier than originally scheduled and some later, especially if
the ordering lead times are long.

The question specifics fail to answer relates to the vendor's
capacity. Did he flow enough product into this customer's
plant to support her total demand, as evidenced by the
aggregate sum of specific receipts? If the answer is no, it's
pointless discussing the details of specifics and why some are
late. It's obvious. They should be discussing how to flow more
total product across the customer's receiving dock. But nowhere
in their discussions was rate of flow even mentioned.

It's a fact that if you expedite something through a resource,
something else will slow down—unless there is idle capacity,
of course. But who has idle capacity they can and do turn on
overnight? The answer: very few. Remember, capacity decisions are not made lightly or quickly; they're expensive. So
expediting something through a resource will cause another
specific item to be made later. This is true even though we
share a wonderful misconception with vendors that when we
expedite our orders it won't be our other orders that suffer, it

will be someone else's. Where did this crazy idea come from? It's ridiculous! And even if it were true, when the other customers expedite, shouldn't we expect some of our specific orders to be delayed? This misconception about vendors means we only talk specifics with them, not flow rates; hence we treat the symptoms and not the disease.

The same problem exists within the factory. Shortage meetings are held regularly, in many plants daily, in some even twice a day. The whole emphasis is on specifics: what parts are on the critical list, and when will they be produced? No one even mentions the term "flow rate." But the same problem that occurs in a vendor's plant—that expediting one thing causes a delay of another—occurs in our own. The worst case is when a resource cannot produce enough, in other words has inadequate capacity. It will always create shortages. The best that expediting can do in this case is to make the capacity problem worse, causing even more shortages. Split lots, uneconomical sequences, and the destruction of the morale of the workers will waste capacity on setups and changeovers, and reduce efficiency and productive hours worked.

The next traps, of course, are our old friends the inventory variables and lead times. With a capacity problem, shortages occur. The solution to shortages is safety stock ("Johnny Carson syndrome"). More orders are triggered to compete for the tight capacity, and hence lead times must extend. We are now deep in the trap of reducing the effective flow rate when the demonstrated flow rate is too small. Inventories start to build, large capacity additions are authorized, and customer service deteriorates. We add overhead and confusion to the factory, so productivity and margins drop just as we need the profits to finance the inventories and capacity additions. How's that for managing a business to increase return on investment? And I'll leave you to think about what effect increasing inventories at the plant has on its suppliers.

The fabrication and assembly industry is characterized by its need to have matched sets of parts. To make a car you must have a body, chassis, engine, transmission, wheels, etc. If you get all these specific parts, except one, in sufficient volume, you cannot assemble and ship. The only thing you have accomplished is a buildup of inventories in the plant. Any time inventories in a plant—either raw materials or work in process— increase, it's a clear sign of a dangerous problem.

What does inventory buildup tell you? It tells me there are some demonstrated flow-rate problems. Demands were placed on these resources, maybe inventory-amplified demands, that exceeded their ability to produce. So choices were made concerning which specific items to make. These decisions were based on the last urgent phone call from a favorite customer or the call from a customer's president whose brother-in-law is on your board of directors. Now the effective flow rate through these few resources dropped at the same time as the demonstrated rate was inadequate. All other resources kept producing at the required rate of flow, inflating material and work-in-process stocks to no avail. The only effect was additional inventory amplification. But at what cost? It's obvious that a correction will occur. When it does, suppliers will be forced to reduce shipments while the factory lives off the bloated stocks.

I hope it's clear that the amplification of demands from distribution systems occurs in synchronization with the amplification of demands from factory inventory systems. The inventories of distributors, manufacturers, and retailers all rise and fall together. The impact on raw-material producers is devastating.

Specifics versus Flow Rates

Specifics and flow rates are so intertwined it is sometimes difficult to untangle them. But untangle them we must. As long as we leave them mixed up, we will always chase specifics, whether they are the cure for the disease or simply the symptoms. And as long as we chase specifics we will vary inventories, amplifying the demand stream throughout the economy.

All knowledgeable practitioners concerned with the planning and scheduling of a factory know that two elements are needed to be successful. These are

1. The planning and control of flow rates (capacity).
2. The planning and control of specifics (priority).

These two points apply as much to outside work centers (vendors) as they do to inside ones. But few practitioners actually consider these two items. Some attempt to plan flow rates, but they're mostly optimists.

There is a big difference between the theoretical flow rate of a resource and what the resource is consistently capable of doing. There is also a lot of pressure to get more through a resource than ever before to show an increase in productivity and, of course, to improve profits. Hence optimism, not realism, is the prevailing emotion.

Let's assume that absenteeism has been running 5 percent on the average last year, but we will plan for 3 percent. Maybe it will get better, we tell ourselves. Efficiency has been running at 82 percent but we are budgeted for 87 percent. We'll use 87 percent in the calculation. Scrap has been 5 percent but we'll plan on 2 percent. We can't afford 5 percent. Rework has been 10 percent but the budget is for only 7 percent. We'll use the budgeted numbers. All the other factors such as machine breakdowns, indirect-to-direct labor ratios, and idle time that affect your real capability to flow product are evaluated the same way, with significant improvements in the expected level of each one. But what's the chance of getting all these improvements simultaneously? Slim to none. If we did, we would be recording significant productivity gains in this country. But for the past several years, productivity gains have been almost zero. An even more important question is, "How many people have a defined program of action with timetables, responsibilities, and measurements to ensure getting these improvements?" Or are productivity gains, as in most plants, simply hopes?

But what about control of flow rates? The word "control" means measuring the actual occurrence against the plan, identifying significant deviations, and doing something to correct the problem. But as we discussed earlier in this chapter, how many plants actually measure flow rates? The answer: ridiculously few, especially among hard-goods producers. As soon as capacity plans are made, usually once a year, they say, "Thank goodness that job's done. Now let's go expedite a specific." If this were not true, your supervisors and buyers would answer your questions about flow rates instead of giving you an answer about specifics. And flow-rate deviation is so simple to measure. Tons, hours, dollars, or units produced can all be compared with planned rates of production. Significant deviations need quick action to ensure that actual flow rates meet the plan so specifics production has a chance.

And now we get to "plan and control specifics." Here's where we shine. Our development of techniques and systems has concentrated on our traditional love affair with specifics. Material requirements planning (MRP) is a formal shortage list system, telling us when we need a specific something. It is a dynamic system, reacting to all changes, whether internally generated (scrap, engineering changes, or incorrect records) or externally (customer request or government regulation).

Shop floor control takes the specifics information from MRP and breaks it down into more refined specifics for each work center. Again it is a dynamic system, reacting to changes with revised specifics. So we plan specifics through our inventory systems, either manually or with computers, and chase them with great vigor, again either manually with hot lists and red tags, or using a computer system.

Vendor rating systems, a normal part of any good purchase order system, also favor specifics. They keep track of what items are late—in other words, what has not yet been delivered—but rarely report how much was delivered early, and even rarer, the total delivered compared with the plan.

These systems are large, expensive attacks on specifics with the traditional bias toward shortages. Little or nothing in these systems provides flow-rate information even though the systems are capable of it. As we have found out, you have to be sure you're getting enough (demonstrated flow rate equals required flow rate) before you have a chance of getting the right things at the right time (effective flow rate equals demonstrated flow rate). So our emphasis has to change. We must throw off our traditional fixation on specifics and instead look more intently at flow rates.

Refinery Analogy

To help us get away from this specifics emphasis, let's look at our factory as if it were a refinery. All resources can be visualized as pipes that flow products through the plant. Vendors are pipes that flow products into the plant. At times we store the products in containers, simulated as tanks. These are our stockrooms and warehouses.

Figure 5-5 shows this analogy clearly. The last pipe is the one delivering product from the plant to the customer, related to our master production schedule.

This is a simple analogy and not completely accurate. Few of our factories are organized so cleanly, as most have functional layouts. Products, especially during the fabrication phase, bounce erratically between the pipes. And it's because of this complexity that we take our eyes off the rates of flow and put them instead on specifics. If you conceptualize your plant as a refinery, its whole management becomes clearer.

The key idea to focus on is the flow rate. Your direct-labor people operating the machines in a given work center are able to flow a certain rate of products to the next work center. Now and again the flow goes into a tank, to await further processing in the case of raw materials and parts, or delivery to a customer in the case of finished goods.

It now becomes obvious that to avoid problems the diameter of the pipes must be planned and the flow rates controlled. Flowmeters must be installed in each pipe to measure whether the actual flow matches the plan and to enforce a match. If the actual flow through one pipe is less than the plan and cannot be increased or supplemented by other pipes, then this one pipe will constrain the whole system.

It's only after the flow rates are balanced that the specifics become interesting. If too much is flowing through any one pipe, all that is being accomplished is inventory building. The correction, either to increase all other pipes significantly or to decrease the diameter of this pipe and all its feeding pipes until the excess inventory is worked off, will have to come sooner or later.

If too little is flowing through any one pipe, inventory is also building because the others are flowing relatively too fast. Excesses and shortages now occur at the same time. The shortages become priorities which can never be valid until the flow rates are rebalanced. And shortages cause inventory variables to change, causing even more shortages.

A key motto is, "If you can't make enough, you can't make the right things at the right time." The best you can do, by

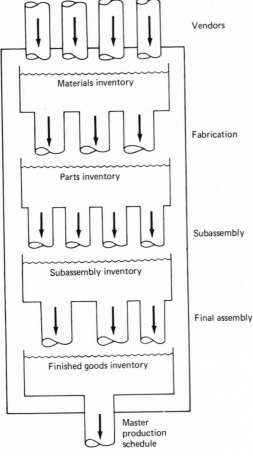

Fig. 5-5 Refinery analogy.

chasing priorities, is aggravate the whole problem, which is capacity, and build inventories. And how many of you have been doing this throughout your career? The split lots, uneconomical sequences, and poor morale of the workers diminish the flow rates, guaranteeing more shortages tomorrow. And to compound the problem, guess which resources get this "favored" treatment? Of course, it is the bottleneck or critical resources, those that pace the total factory's output. Imagine the financial gains if the critical rate-limiting resources produced just 2 percent more with the same people and assets as you have today. That is a 2 percent increase in shipments with the same fixed costs, sure to make a significant contribution to your company's profit or loss statement.

The education program necessary to get this message across is overwhelming. Company presidents, general managers, sales managers, plant superintendents, supervisors, production people, and inventory control people are all guilty of a specifics focus. Now you really see where the neck of the bottle is—at the top!

The terrible consequence of a failure to recognize a flow-rate constraint is inventory building. And all factories are constrained by capacity at some point, whether the capacity of people, the machinery, or the physical plant. The magnitude and timing of the constraint depend on your access to money. But inventory is also money, tied up largely in nonproductive uses. And it makes no sense when there is a flow-rate constraint and all the cash we can get is needed to solve it, to tie up more cash in inventory. But that, my friends, is exactly what we do.

Consider the following dialogue between some key people in a manufacturing company. You might find yourself in this conversation or know someone who's taking part in it.

Sales manager: I've just booked this big new order for fast delivery. (Why can't they ever sell what we have or give the factory the needed time to produce efficiently?)

Master scheduler: But our capacity is already oversold. (There's always somebody being negative. Get on the winning team and be positive!)

General manager: Nonsense! This factory can make twice as much as we are now. (Oh, why can't we separate the theoretical capacity of a factory from its practical level today?)

Finance director: And look at the profits if we ship on time. (Yes, those gross margins are nice on incremental sales, aren't they? But the factory has to produce it to ship it, and we only get paid after shipment, not when the order is booked.)

Manufacturing manager: Just get the work on the shop floor; we'll push it through. (There's "Superexpediter" at work, ready to "leap long queues in a single bound." No question this job gets highest priority, at least until the next hot job comes along. And *this* job might get shipped on time, but what about the others already booked and promised to customers?)

Master scheduler: But our capacity is already oversold. . . .

Conversations like this are all too common, no matter what the economic conditions. Plant capacity is usually sized to the needs of the marketplace or slightly less. Add a sudden increase in demand without a corresponding increase in capacity and shortages grow. Priorities start changing frequently as we jump from one hot job to another. The results are poor customer service; factory disruption, hence productivity loss; and inventory growth.

To compound the problem, now inventory variables and lead times enter the picture. Emotion also takes over, and the devastating cycle of buying and making the wrong things starts, at some time to be replaced by a severe inventory correction. The classical boom-and-bust cycle occurs in miniature.

The refinery analogy shows this clearly. Assume customer demand has increased a little but capacity has not kept pace. Emotion, priorities, inventory techniques, and systems take over. Flow rates are not increased. Instead a number of the items produced are the wrong ones. Even more things are ordered now as we chase priorities. Safety stocks are boosted, and the levels in the tanks increase. Vendors see an amplified demand and repeat the cycle in their factories. Total inventories and shortages grow at the same time. Our shipments drop because we fail to get sets of parts that match.

This scenario even occurs when business is bad. Many purchasing people tell me their deliveries from vendors are worse during a slowdown than when business is booming. The reason? Vendor capacity is reduced more than business conditions warrant, and there is a great reluctance to add costs when business is bad. So delivery performance suffers at the very time it should be the best.

We get back in balance when capacities are increased enough to overpower the shortages. (That is when the demonstrated flow rate is far higher than the required rate.) But now inventories start to grow alarmingly, our lead times reduce, and customers start to cancel, so we reduce our production schedules. Layoffs and short work weeks occur. We live off our bloated inventories, so the vendors now see an almost complete cessation of ordering from us. They are forced to repeat this cycle in their plants. And they hope the next boom will come before they run out of cash or credit and have to close up shop.

Chapter Six

Inventory as a Dampener

Ask the average person on the street this question: "What role should inventory play when demand for products oscillates?" After some thought the invariable answer will be, "To act as a dampener. To absorb the peaks and valleys of demand and allow the supplier to operate with a level schedule." Sounds nice and logical, doesn't it? In practice it's just the opposite. Inventories amplify the peaks and valleys of demand into huge shock waves on all businesses and through our economy. And a lot of this amplification is done with theoretically correct techniques, many of them programmed into big computers, that fail to consider the aggregate impact. And don't forget that wonderful human override, emotion. If the system and techniques don't louse it up, people will for sure.

Consider the pressure that financial people exert on inventories. When business is bad, inventories must be cut to free up cash to finance debt because profits are not adequate. When sales are healthy, the lid comes off inventories and we are allowed to increase them. Even our measurements of inventory reflect this emphasis. We talk about days' supply or inventory turnover, linking inventories in both cases to demand. So when business is bad we decrease inventories to keep these ratios at desirable levels and in so doing shut off demand to our suppliers. When business is good, inventories are allowed to increase, meaning that we put extra demands on our suppliers over and above the true demand increase we are experiencing. "Return on investment," that wonderful measure of business performance, also forces the same oscillation in inventories, again exactly at the wrong time. So there's no incentive to dampen fluctuations, but many incentives to amplify them.

The Great Bathtub Mystery

No, I am not converting this book into an Agatha Christie–type novel. I am talking about the management of inventories. We must see inventory for what it is: a level of product in a bathtub. Products flow into the bathtub as a result of procurement or manufacturing decisions. They flow out when shipments are made. The analogy can be used for the total economy, for a complete corporation, for just one plant or distributor, or even for segments of inventory such as work-in-process inventory. Figure 6-1 shows the bathtub for a manufacturer. Two pipes—purchases and direct labor—flow product into the bathtub. One pipe—shipments—drains it.

Pictures similar to this can be drawn for segments of inventory. The total bathtub for a manufacturer can be broken into several bathtubs, as in Figure 6-2. Stocks of raw materials

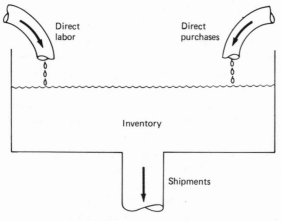

Fig. 6-1 Inventory bathtub.

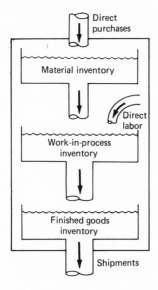

Fig. 6-2   Inventory bathtub segments.

and purchased parts have only one inflow pipe—purchases—
and the outflow pipe represents issues to the factory.

Work-in-process inventory has two inflow pipes: (1) the
outflow from stores of raw materials and purchased parts and
(2) the direct labor. The outflow pipe is either shipments
directly to a customer or deliveries to a warehouse.

Finished goods inventories, whether they are at a central, a
regional, or a local warehouse, have only one inflow pipe,
deliveries either from the manufacturer or from the upstream
distribution point. The single outflow pipe is deliveries to the
downstream needs, either another warehouse in the distribution chain, the retail store, or the end customer.

It is now clear how inventory amplifies real demand. Small
increases in outflow (real demand) accompanied by a simultaneous desire to increase the level of water in the bathtub
(safety-stock and lot-size increases) force the increase in inflow
to be larger than the increase in outflow. It's as simple as that.

A multistage distribution network takes each increased
demand and amplifies it more. It does the converse on the
way down. Multistage manufacturing operates the same way.

Feeder plants and user plants are linked together the same way as a distribution network. Downstream factories amplify the small demand increases into large increases on the upstream plants because changed inventory parameters are trying to deepen the level in the bathtub. Again the reverse occurs with reduced demand.

This is a critical point. When inventories are increasing, the only question to keep asking yourself is, "When will they start decreasing?" The correction *will* come; the only question is when. And with the correction, all the problems of layoffs and idle machinery originally added to support the fictitious demand caused by inventory building will also come.

Depending on where you are in the logistics chain, this building of inventory and subsequent destocking is either a severe or a minor problem. Raw-material producers, for example steel mills or aluminum producers, are in the worst place. They are at the beginning of the supply chain and hence get whiplashed the most with inventory cycles. Distributors and retailers of consumer products, because they are closest to the real demand, are affected least by these changes.

The whole problem is accentuated by time lags in the system. A manufacturer sees a slightly increased rate of customer orders. The factory will not or cannot react as fast with capacity to support these orders. The manufacturer thinks, "Well, you know, business has been bad (assuming we are at the bottom of the bust cycle) so we don't want to incur unnecessary costs. Bringing people back from layoff too early means we will have to lay them off again or carry them on the payroll. Both actions cost us money we cannot afford. And we don't know if this is a temporary condition or a permanent one. It could be simply a time shift in customers placing orders (the purchasing agent is going on vacation so is trying to get ahead of the work load).

The manufacturer doesn't know if it's a permanent or a temporary change and thus figures, "Let's wait and see for a while what happens. We're probably unproductive at these operating rates anyhow, so maybe the factory will be able to handle the increased business with the people they've got." I hope you see the seeds of the lead-time syndrome in these comments.

When incoming orders exceed your capacity there are only a few choices.

1. Refuse the orders. Who's going to do that, especially when business is bad to start with? Why, that's almost un-American.
2. Increase capacity quickly. This could be costly if it's only a temporary increase or future business ordered early.
3. Take the order and lie to your customers. Promise them deliveries you probably cannot meet. But don't forget, your late deliveries will function as effectively as increased lead times to stimulate fictitious demand.
4. Increase lead times. Why not? It seems the safest thing to do under the circumstances and will let you wait and see how things are shaping up before company resources are committed.

However, in reality no one refuses orders when business is bad. Neither do they increase capacity rapidly, so we can forget the first two options.

Most companies lie to their customers where delivery promises are concerned. If they didn't, customer service levels achieved by manufacturers around the world would be approaching 100 percent. But they aren't, not by a long shot. An average of 75 percent would probably be closer to the mark. So the third option is a distinct possibility. But don't forget the cautionary rule that goes with this option.

The fourth choice appears to be such a logical solution, and so painless. It doesn't commit any company resources, the order is received, customers are not lied to, and time is provided to wait and see what will really happen.

But do you see how stupid such an action is? "Let's wait and see how things are shaping up before company resources are committed." What will increasing lead times do to the order flow rates? Increase them of course! How can this possibly be of help to "see how things are shaping up?" This simple action just destroyed any chance you had of seeing how things are "shaping up." Combine this with the inventory variables now being manipulated downstream from your plant—when lead times increase, buy more sooner (emotion talking); when lead times increase, update the computer so it can

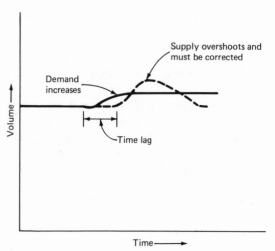

Fig. 6-3 Supply changes lagging demand changes.

mathematically adjust safety stock (techniques at work)—and away we go. Fictitious demands now hit constrained capacity, surely the worst scenario you can imagine.

Supply changes lagging behind demand shift, and the subsequent effect on the industrial world, were described many years ago by Jay Forrester in his book *Industrial Dynamics*. He showed that information about small demand increases takes time to flow to the supply pipes. When supply reacts, the reaction must be more severe and then tends to overshoot the real demand increase. Forrester used computer simulations to show how this time-lag effect could make supply changes oscillate dramatically even though demand changes were slight. This can be seen in Figure 6-3. Combine this with inventory oscillation and our reticence to change capacity and you see the amplification problem clearly.

In order for inventory to act as a dampener, or at least be neutral, instead of acting as an amplifier, significant change is required in all our theories, systems, and management of inventories, in addition to our measures of business health. The current state of the art of these systems is not designed to force inventories out of the amplification business.

Demand Management

Let's look at a multitier production and distribution chain. It can be visualized as a series of bathtubs linked together as in Figure 6-4. The example shows seven factories and distributors in this chain, probably fewer than the average.

We have already seen how inventory management practices

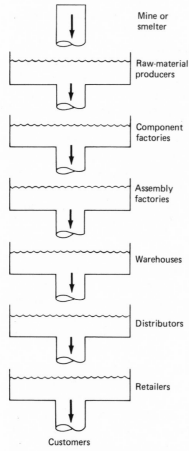

Mine or
smelter

Raw-material
producers

Component
factories

Assembly
factories

Warehouses

Distributors

Retailers

Customers

Fig. 6-4   Multitier logistics chain.

take small changes in demand from customers and convert these changes into huge production variations for the raw-material producers. The attempt to increase the levels of inventory in all the bathtubs is the culprit.

We have also seen how lead time, especially the stacked lead time for the total economy, influences the quality of the product flows, that is, the right things in the right quantity at the right time. Figures 5-1 and 5-2 showed the problem that arises when effective flow rates drop, causing demonstrated flow rates to increase above the required rates. So now the question is, "How do we prevent this? How do we make inventory a dampener of demand oscillations?"

The first key is that the flow rates between the various elements in the chain must be matched and controlled to suit the average end-customer demand. As soon as flow rates are pegged to end demand, inventory ceases to be an amplifier. It can only function then as a dampener of specific peaks and valleys of demand. These flow rates must be quickly responsive to average demand changes to avoid draining or filling one or more bathtubs excessively. With this scenario, when customer demand increases 3 percent, all elements in the chain will increase their flow rates 3 percent. We will not get 3 percent customer demand becoming 81 percent increased demand at the factory as we do with inventory amplification.

This scenario is a totally new concept for most factories and distributors. First it assumes that all elements in the production and supply chain measure and control their outputs to match average end-customer demand. This sounds easy, but how can it be done? How does a producer of a product, especially of raw materials, know what the end-customer demand really is? This producer is too far removed from the end customer with too many pockets of inventory intervening to get a good reading. But some companies *do* keep track of end-user demand or at least try to. Whether they use the information effectively or not is another question.

Some manufacturers manage the inventories of their products throughout the distribution chain, including at the retail store. They know exactly what the end demand is because their inventory management system records the sales. They control the inventory levels at their distributors and decide on their replenishment. With this information it is easy to set operating rates to match real needs. But these companies are in the minority and only do this for their big customers. They could still get whiplashed by their small customers. To avoid this problem they usually apply the demand changes of big customers to their small ones on a pro rata basis. Of course, the marketing people reading this will say that these companies could be losing business. All big customers were once small. Maybe some of these small customers are performing significantly better than the average, and this could be true. A failure to produce enough for these small aggressive companies could be a serious mistake. Although I bow to this wisdom, the terrible and more damaging problem is to have inventory whiplash your business. I hope that those small companies which outperform the norm can be handled by exception.

Other companies use the warranty or liability card as their measure of true demand. Many products, especially consumer goods, include in the product package a card asking you to register the product with the company. This is said to be for the consumer's protection in case of product defects and the need for recalls. They ask other information on the card, such as sex, age, and income, and they use this information not only for marketing but to get clean sales statistics. If a company has experienced a historical return rate for their cards, then it's easy to convert the number of cards returned into actual sales. This is especially helpful to producers insulated from end customers by a lengthy multitier distribution network not under their control.

Of course this only picks up actual sales. If the retailer is out of stock and customers are forced to buy competitors' products, these cards will not indicate that. If the retailer wants to build up inventory of this item because he has it featured in a promotion, again the cards don't show that. So some knowledge of field stocks and their planned changes is needed to be able to use this mechanism effectively.

Still other companies have regular meetings with a group of their largest distributors to discuss end-product sales and inventory strategies being used by both the distributors and the manufacturer, and to jointly develop decisions on production volumes to meet the real demand.

In all cases the objective is to set plant operating rates to suit real demand. Inventories are not allowed to create the amplifier effect. When total flow rate is set, the only remaining question is how to allocate products, as they are made, to the various distribution channels.

When real demand changes are seen, the question becomes how to react. Is it a permanent or a temporary change in demand? If it's permanent, the first question is how to get the flow rates from the plant to equal the changed sales. If the change is an increase in demand, the change in plant flow rates will usually take some time. The inventories in the system must be used to provide time to react. Forcing the inventories throughout the system to *drop* provides this time. Production must now exceed real demand to rebuild the depleted stocks. If the time lag is long, production will need to be significantly above the demand rate for a while before it then falls back to the average demand as illustrated in Figure 6-3. You see now why a fast reaction to a change in flow rates is so critical.

If the demand change is a decrease, then flow rates must be adjusted downward. This is usually a quicker task, although not always, especially if you are trying to keep a stable work force of skilled people or the process is inefficient at reduced output rates. Inventory building is the result of not reducing flow rates quickly and is certain to need correcting sometime in the future. If demand has decreased permanently, the only two ways to cut inventories are to temporarily drop production below the demand rate or to stimulate an increase in demand through a promotion or price cutting. The latter course is only effective if it results in an actual increase in demand. The problem is that it often results in selling future business today at a lower sales price, not a very smart business decision.

If the real demand changes are temporary, the objective should be to let flow rates stay constant and force the inventory to cushion them. If the demand increases, then the inventories should be forced to drop, and if demand decreases, then inventories should be built up. But this approach is so contrary to current thinking, technology, systems, and measurements! The only place it works to a certain degree is with inventories of foodstuffs and our country's strategic reserves. Both are normally built up in periods when supply exceeds demand

and depleted when demand exceeds supply. But then, the government has no return on investment measure to stop inventories from being, in this case, so very logical.

I mentioned earlier that there are no techniques designed to implement this philosophy. That is not quite true. In the distribution area, several companies use what is called "push" distribution. This literally means, produce a volume of product and push it to the warehouses. Companies that run their own distribution networks use this philosophy. The allocation formula, sometimes called "fair shares" allocation, sends an amount to a warehouse based on its share of the total sales and current inventory position.

But companies with separate distribution channels, which are in the majority, usually use "pull" distribution. This is the classic inventory replenishment mechanism with all the inventory theory built right in. This is why our total economy is whiplashed as badly as it is. Few companies push; most companies pull.

The push philosophy is also rarely followed between feeder and user plants, even those in the same company. Decisions concerning inventories at the user plant simply show up as changed demand at the feeder plant. These either result in changed output rates at the feeder plant or changed lead times quoted back to the user plant. In no way are the flow rates balanced.

One company I know has several user plants linked to two feeders. The feeders go through the classic boom-and-bust cycle even though all their production is used by downstream plants of the same company. Recently the feeder plants received more orders than their capacity could support. Lead times extended, and they started missing deliveries because their estimate of real capacity was too high. The backlog of past-due orders started increasing rapidly. This combination of events triggered more orders from all the user plants.

The feeders set up a program to increase capacity significantly because of the heat they were getting from the corporation for poor performance and because of their large and growing order book. Their capacity program was very successful. They started to eat quickly into the order book and their past-due orders. This increased flow rate affected the user plants by causing inventory increases (what else?). *They* were getting heat from the corporation to trim stocks, so they shut off ordering from the feeders. This was possible because of the reduced lead times now being quoted and their high inventories. In a matter of a few months, the feeder plants were laying off workers and shutting down some of their production lines, at significant cost to the corporation.

Another company I know even wrote several years ago a booklet entitled "The Internal Business Cycle" and distributed it to all key managers. It exactly described the conditions we have discussed. But the company has no mechanism in place to stop the effects of the cycle. Their feeder plants are still being whiplashed by the user plants as they tinker with the inventory techniques.

The same flow-rate approach described for manufacturer and distributor can work between user and feeder plants. And they do not have to be in the same corporation; they can be separate companies.

The first thing to do is to establish and contract for flow rates. These should be based on *real* average demand at the user plant or at least the best guess of what this will be. They should be in capacity terms, for example, tons, units by product family, dollars, or standard hours. Once these are set, the only question left is which specific items make up this flow rate. These items can be decided short range, as few products really take a long time to make. This is similar to the fair shares allocation process described earlier, but in this case it's a capacity allocation process, detailed at the last minute for specific quantities of specific items at a specific time.

If real demand changes, then flow rates must be adjusted quickly to suit it. Delays will either create the lead-time syndrome or build excess inventory, both certain to cause severe problems for both parties. With flow rates balanced and a short decision time for specifics, effective capacity (making the right quantity of the right parts at the right time) is high, and total inventories are very low with no amplification possibility.

Our techniques and systems will need changing to implement the push philosophy. The focus must be changed from specifics to flow rates to provide the necessary information for the capacity contract. It's our only chance to stop the inventory amplification cycle from destroying our financial performance. Thus a different set of data must be used as the communication mechanism between user and feeder facilities. The traditional methods, purchase orders and sales orders, cannot define flow rates. They are specifics-oriented, not flow-rate-oriented.

Now I have no grand design to organize this philosophy for the total world economy. I am not sure it's possible, and I don't think it's at all desirable. Besides, the centrally planned economies of some parts of the world are certainly no example of a healthy business climate. But as a general manager, you can partially insulate your business from inventory effects. And you can do your part to stop amplifying the demands on your suppliers by avoiding systems that have you push inventory replenishment numbers around.

Changing focus from specifics to flow rates is not easy. I was asked several years ago to discuss the lead-time syndrome with all the customers of a foundry. Bill, the general manager of the foundry, invited all his major customers to a large university near his plant, where I conducted the discussion. He paid the expenses of all his customers (air fares, motel, and meals) plus my fee and expenses. We talked all day about the lead-time syndrome and its terrible side effects.

At the close of the meeting Bill made this offer. He said to his customers, "I don't need long lead times to make castings. I can make any casting you want in a couple of weeks. I know that if I quote you long lead times your guess of what you really want when you want it will be wrong. So you hedge, order more sooner, and I lose track of the real demand. So here's my suggestion. Give me a feel of the flow rates you need over the next 3 months. It should preferably be based on your finished goods production schedule or, failing that, based on your ability to consume castings. (It's obvious that if your 40 direct labor machinists have consumed an average of 1 ton of castings per week in the past and there are no plans to increase the number of workers or the total hours worked, then 1 ton of castings per week is the required flow rate.) Tell me the specifics about the castings (part number, quantity, and date) only on a short-range basis, say, no more than 2 weeks out. I will staff for your flow rates, have materials for your flow rates, and produce specifics quickly from these resources to suit your needs."

Now you may wonder why a vendor is pushing this hard for flow rates. What's in it for him? Well in this case, the boom-and-bust cycle of 1974 to 1975 almost threw this company into bankruptcy. They expanded in 1974 because of the huge order book they were carrying, but the crash of 1975 hit them just as the order book was being completed. The sales dried up and cash flow and profits were inadequate to pay for the debt they took on to finance the expansion. They suffered terribly for quite some time. And, in this case, the general manager is also a major stockholder. He almost saw his life's work destroyed. At significant cost the plant survived. He wanted flow-rate information to prevent anything like this from happening again. It was a purely defensive move.

I called him 3 months later. I said, "Bill, how's your program going? How many customers have signed up? What delivery performance are you achieving? Are your customers pleased with the program?"

He replied, "I've yet to get the first one even interested. You see, lead times are short now, so the purchasing people want to shop around, find the best prices, and do some high-level negotiating. They're not interested in being locked into a contract for flow rates." (We'll come back to this comment about being locked in later.)

I said, "Well, keep trying, Bill. Let me know if I can help."

I called again 6 months later, 9 months after the initial discussion. I asked, "Bill, how're we doing? How's your track record? How many customers are now signed up?"

He said, "I've yet to get the first one interested. I'm quoting 6 to 8 weeks' lead time, and they would rather put that in their systems and send me purchase orders for specifics."

Put yourself in Bill's shoes right now. What are his choices if incoming orders start to increase? One is to add capacity. But he doesn't know if his order increase is real demand or fictitious demand triggered by inventory systems manipulating the data on specifics. And he was burned by that in 1974 to 1975.

Another choice is to hold capacity constant and simply quote longer lead times. He knows this will trigger increased orders, but as long as he operates his constant capacity efficiently it won't hurt *him*. He will get a lot of flack from his customers, who will have severe shortages, but that's unlikely to affect his current orders. Where else can his customers go when lead times from all domestic foundries are long? Overseas is the only place. And of course that's where they go, damaging our economy by letting imports make up the capacity loss instead of causing domestic production to increase. The correct choice, to communicate and balance flow rates, was denied him by his customers' desire to "shop around" and be flexible.

Many companies do operate with flow rates as their primary concern with specifics a secondary one. Many process industries are classic examples of how effective this approach is. The sheer volume of products flowing and the relatively few items they produce force this kind of thinking. But as soon as the physical volume is not that high and the variety increases (the typical fabrication and assembly manufacturer or industrial distributor), this kind of outlook is supplanted by one that focuses on specifics.

Wrong Paperwork

A large share of the blame for our failure to discuss flow rates with each other is our current way of communicating business needs. Most ordering and commitment activities occur with sales orders and purchase orders. These orders state a need or a promise for a specific item and a specific quantity to be delivered on a specific date. In the average company thousands of these orders are placed or received each month. But no one looks at their aggregate effect on flow rates. The people placing purchase orders have no idea what total demands they are making on each vendor. The flow rates implied by all these purchase orders are simply not calculated.

Vendors may have a good idea of the total flow rate all their customer orders represent for their businesses, but they have little if any knowledge of what flow rate each customer requires and whether it's reasonable or not.

Pur:hase orders and sales orders should cease to be the primary communication vehicles. They should become secondary to a flow-rate agreement. You simply split the agreed flow rate into specifics short term. When flow rates are agreed to and are in balance, there are few specific items that cannot be made in a couple of weeks.

Now I am sure some of you are thinking that not all things can be planned this way. That's true; this is not a panacea. But a huge amount of buying and selling can be done this way as soon as we feel it's worthwhile. And I hope I have proved to you that it's worthwhile.

People's Objections

We are so used to talking to each other about purchase orders and sales orders—the language of specifics—that all functions and management levels will resist the suggestion to think in terms of flow rates. Let's look at some of the objections you'll hear and see if they're valid.

"A flow-rate contract is more of a commitment than purchase orders for specifics."

Is that really true? Purchase orders are contracts for part numbers, quantities, and dates. We can only cancel or change them if the vendor allows. Of course the vendor allows it to get our business. But here we are making long-term contracts for specifics, which are sure to be wrong. Aren't these orders in total a picture of the flow rate required? Of course they are. Just look at Figure 6-5. This is the file drawer where the vendor keeps customers' orders. (I apologize to all the computer experts who would rather see this as a spinning disk or magnetic tape, but sometimes old-fashioned pictures make better analogies.) You have several orders for specifics in this file drawer, intermingled with other customers' orders. What

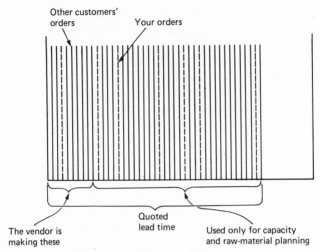

Fig. 6-5   Vendor's file drawer.

is the vendor doing with your orders for specifics? In the majority of cases, nothing, except using them to plan capacity. The specifics order is only removed in the short term, when the start of its actual production lead time is reached. Up to that point the specifics orders simply serve to inform the vendor of capacity, and of which lead time to quote. So here you are contracting for wrong specifics (the triple-forecast error problem) so the vendor can plan capacity. Why not let capacity be planned directly without the intermediate wrong step? You are less, not more, committed with a flow-rate contract in relation to the vendor's quoted lead time than you are with purchase orders for specifics. With a flow-rate contract at least you have infinite flexibility relative to specifics. And if purchase orders can be canceled or changed, why not a flow-rate contract? Doesn't the vendor still want your business? Of course the vendor does.

"I want to shop around and find the best prices for my company. I don't want to be locked in."

This certainly is a concern. One of purchasing's major activities is saving money with better prices. But that function is also overrated. Buyers do *not* change vendors often. For starters, many items, such as castings, forgings, or specialty sheet metal items, need special tooling. The specifications or qualification procedures for other items prohibit switching vendors easily. And does a flow-rate contract prevent switching vendors? Of course not. It does limit short-term changes, but so do purchase orders placed over an 8-week or longer horizon. In the longer term other vendors can be selected if they have better prices or conditions.

"A flow-rate contract is not as binding and specific as a purchase order. What if the vendor doesn't treat it as a valid order and I get out of his queue? Now what?"

Well, in that case you would be out of the vendor's queue, and you would not get the parts you needed when you needed them. But why won't the vendor treat the flow-rate contract with as much faith as a purchase order? If you were the sales or general manager of the vendor's plant, which document would you be more interested in, a purchase order defining a delivery of a specific item or a contract defining a weekly rate of flow to the customer? I know which one I'd be more pleased with.

"I'll no longer have a big healthy backlog of orders. How can I book a flow-rate contract into my system with no part numbers, quantities, and dates? What do I tell my board of directors or shareholders?"

Well, one way to solve this problem is to create a fictitious product number and average price for the flow-rate contract. Let this be entered into the system and—voilà—an order book to please the spectators. Of course another—and a better—choice is to educate those around you in the value of this way of working.

"Customers are going to be allocated product? What if they want more and the factory can't increase capacity? Does that mean I can't take more orders? Don't forget I'm paid on commission so this will affect my pocketbook directly."

This is probably the toughest comment to handle. Salespeople are competitive and want nothing to do with schemes that seem to hurt their ability to book orders. They are probably the single largest group preventing this approach from gaining wider acceptance.

But as we have seen, taking orders for specifics whiplashes the economy and each business. And it's not taking orders that generates commissions (or shouldn't be), it's shipments. Why else do salespeople expedite their orders through the plant?

If boom-and-bust cycles continue, won't they in reality hurt the salesperson's pocketbook in total more severely? I know this means taking a long-term view, but that's the only one that makes any sense. If we can size the flow rates correctly and handle small real changes in demand successfully, don't we make the salesperson's job easier and more productive, resulting in increased commissions? Most failures to increase capacity to suit customers' needs occur when the inventory whiplash is at work, certainly not when capacity changes are related to true demand. Get the pipes flowing to suit actual demand and the number of occurrences of inadequate capacity will drop almost to zero. And with flow rates clearly conveyed from user to supplier, logical capacity expansions can be justified to handle the real increases in business.

"You mean I can't decide how much inventory to carry in my warehouse? Some turkey at the corporate offices is going to decide for me? I'm measured on customer service in my territory as well as return on investment. If I haven't got the goods, how can I perform?"

You must take responsibility for inventory decisions away from individual departments like warehouses. This may mean a realignment of your organization, responsibilities, and measurements. If you have multiple responsibilities for inventories, then the inventory whiplash will always occur.

Realignment is not difficult when you own both the manufacturing and the distribution networks. The push distribution and fair shares allocation described earlier are the mechanisms. When it's difficult is when product ownership changes hands at each link. In this case we have to hope that we can get the level of cooperation needed for this idea to work. This is probably not completely possible, so the economy will always seesaw back and forth a little. But maybe if enough people see the light, the cycles will be less vicious.

"You mean I can't use my state-of-the-art inventory control system to make ordering decisions for me? I've just spent a fortune on new hardware and software and you're telling me its no good."

That's exactly right. Use your fancy new system and you'll fail to manage inventory, unless you incorporate additional controls to force the system to perform using the concepts we've been describing. We'll talk about that some more in Chapter 9, but material requirements planning (MRP), distribution requirements planning (DRP) or just plain order point–order quantity replenishment systems are all designed to focus attention on specifics—part number, quantity, and date—not on flow rates. And it's flow rates we need to know about first; specifics come later.

As you can see, we have a tremendous education problem. General managers, sales, purchasing, finance, manufacturing, warehousing, production, inventory control, and systems people all need to understand their roles in solving this problem. All are affected by it and all contribute to it. It will take all of them to solve it.

We must also educate the economists and business writers who are saying that when order flow rates are higher than shipments, the economy is healthy. We must stop them from focusing on backlogs of orders and making judgments about our economy if the backlogs are increasing or decreasing. Bank managers, investors, and all people interested in the movement of goods through our economy need to understand the basic problems with our traditional way of evaluating performance, whether within a company or in the total economy.

We can no longer talk about an "arms-length" relationship with our customers and vendors. Flow-rate information must pass more often and more clearly between users and suppliers. This means a newer and expanded role for all functions, a subject we will discuss in the next chapter.

Chapter Seven

Input-Output Control

The manufacturing, distribution, and retailing businesses are all very complex, mainly because of the huge number of details they handle. It is estimated that 10 million bits of active information are in use in the average manufacturing plant. Inventory withdrawals and receipts, labor transactions, sales orders, purchasing requisitions and order placements, accounts payable and receivable, bills of materials, and routings are all examples of this data. This volume of information means thousands of small decisions that affect inventory levels are made daily. These decisions range from purchasing actions to sales actions to overtime decisions to job-scheduling procedures.

It should come as no surprise then that these actions are rarely under control. No one clearly sees the total impact of all these small decisions on the business until after the fact. And then it's inventory. Contrast this with the control we have on other expenditures. All departments have budgets for expenses and operating supplies and are measured regularly on achieving these figures. A plant manager, even though he is at a high management level, is not authorized to spend more than a relatively small amount of money on capital investments, say $5000, without approval of the capital appropriations review board. But clerks in most inventory departments can authorize the procurement of $200,000 of direct materials without any approval or review. And deciding that the general manager should sign all purchase orders over a certain dollar figure is not the solution either. How does the general manager know if the product is really needed? Again this focus is on checking a few large specifics. In no way does it control the totals.

But the two different expenditures, capital investments or material procurement, use the same financial resources of the business, and create the same result: assets. One, capital equipment, is usually productive; the other, inventory, is questionable. If the right stuff is ordered and is transformed quickly into a product that's delivered to a customer at a profit, then it's good stuff. But there's a fair risk it will be the wrong stuff, leaving you with one of the most unproductive assets possible.

With this amount of detail the only hope is to summarize. Control can then be exercised over the aggregates and the details forced to match. Top management can then counterbalance the "more" syndrome present in every inventory decision with an equal force, demanding the status quo or even less.

The Great Bathtub Mystery Revisited

Chapter 6 discussed the "great bathtub mystery," but it's no mystery at all. Inventory is something you do not control directly, only indirectly. I always get a kick out of people who tell me their title is "inventory control manager." How can you be a manager of something that by definition cannot be controlled directly? Inventory is whatever is left over, the residue in the bathtub, what you might call the scum on the bottom. And this is an especially good word for most of it, because it's slow moving or obsolete!

What you *can* control is the flow rates into and out of the bathtub. These aggregate flow rates must be controlled to prevent the inventory oscillations that occur far too often. Hoping that the sum of all the thousands of small decisions described earlier equals the aggregate flow rates you desire is ridiculous. There is too much illogic built into our detailed systems, and what this doesn't screw up, our old friend "emotion" will take care of.

So the total flow rates first must be established with details coming second. Details must be forced to fit the totals. This has some profound implications for our current inventory theories, techniques, planning, and scheduling systems. We will cover this in depth in Chapter 9. But it's obvious where current systems fall down: they concentrate on details and ignore totals.

Let's return to the bathtub idea. All inventories can be represented as shown in Figure 6-1. The only difference is whether there is one flow into the bathtub or two. Distributors and retailers usually have just one incoming flow, although sometimes warehouse costs flow into inventory just as a manufacturer flows direct labor into inventory. This is especially true of those distributors who sell individual items as well as kits, for example, engine bearings, tune-up kits, or hand tools. Manufacturers always have two flows, sometimes more, depending on the accounting system they use. To keep the example simple we will only consider either one or two flows into the bathtub. Sometimes the flow out of the bathtub can be split into several flows, especially when manufacturers have a large segment of their output going to an affiliate plant for further processing. But again, to keep it simple, we will only consider one output flow. You should be able to modify the following discussion for the specifics of your situation and the peculiarities of your accounting system.

Is it clear that the control of inventory is the control of the inflow and outflow pipes? I am always amazed how few people understand this. Even fewer people actually have specific management tools in place to *force* the flows to achieve the corporate inventory objectives. It's so easy to do because all the required information is readily available.

The specific management tool needed is called an inventory input-output chart. We will discuss the more complex version, needed by a manufacturer, rather than that used by a warehouse manager or retailer. However, the chart can be easily modified according to your business. Figure 7-1 shows a portion of an input-output chart for a company. The actual chart is for a 12-month period, but only a few months are shown. The

Inventory Jan. 1 = $3,000,000
Goal   Dec. 31 = $2,400,000

Month	Purchased materials			Production labor			Shipments			Inventory		
	Planned	Actual	Deviation	Planned	Actual	Deviation	Planned	Actual	Deviation	Planned	Actual	Deviation
Jan.	240	260	20	160	150	(10)	450	430	(20)	2950	2980	30
Feb.	240	230	(10)	160	165	5	450	470	20	2900	2905	5
Mar.	270	260	(10)	180	175	(5)	500	480	(20)	2850	2860	10
Apr.	270			180			500			2800		
etc.												

Fig. 7-1 Inventory input-output.

latter half of the year could easily be summarized into quarters rather than months.

They have an inventory on January 1 of $3 million with a goal of $2.4 million by December 31. At this stage it's not important where the goal came from; we will discuss that in Chapter 8. It could be the result of calculations (unlikely) or a management edict (probably). But whatever the source, we do know the level in the bathtub is budgeted to drop by $600,000 over a 12-month period. It may sound obvious but the only way to do that is to ship $600,000 more at inventory-relief dollars than is added through purchases and direct labor over the next 12 months. And let me make the point again. Hoping that your detailed inventory system and all the people involved in detailed decisions affecting small pieces of inventory will get you this reduction is ridiculous. It will never happen.

Our plan is to drop the inventory equally over the next 12 months, that is, at a rate of $50,000 per month. This is in contrast to the normal way that inventory behaves: it balloons up in the first half of the fiscal year, plateaus for the third quarter, and then needs rapid reduction in the fourth. Such wonderful edicts as "Shut the receiving dock 2 weeks out of every month," "No overtime allowed in the last quarter," and "Return this stuff to the vendor for a restocking charge," are usually given, sure to shut off the high-volume movers and destroy the first quarter's production next year. And you can visualize, I am sure, the inventory oscillation you are causing for your vendors.

In our scenario, we are going to reduce inventory by $50,000 per month. The first numbers we need are the shipping budgets at cost of goods sold or inventory-relief dollars. This is part of the annual operating plan for most businesses, so it is easily obtained. Since the shipping budget is usually an annual figure, some way of dividing it into months and quarters is needed. Past history of seasonal biases, or a simple linear spread of the numbers if there is no recurrent historical patterns, will do. In our example there is a seasonal pattern which is reflected in the shipments plan.

Subtracting $50,000 from each month's numbers defines how much will be *allowed* to flow in through purchases and labor.

The split between purchases and labor now becomes important. Most financial people keep track of the historical mix of purchases and labor in their product. Provided that the current inventory is not out of balance with this historical mix, these ratios can be applied directly to the incoming flow numbers. In our example, 60 percent for purchases and 40 percent for direct labor have been used, about average in industry. (This does depend on your financial system, of course, and how factory burden is treated.) If the inventory is out of balance, then this condition must be considered in generating the flow-rate numbers. More or less purchased materials or direct labor than the historical mix may be needed for a while until a balance is reestablished.

Performing these simple calculations for each period provides a flow-rate plan for the business. These numbers are all generated during the annual budgeting exercises, so the numbers simply need to be transferred to one piece of paper. And this a critical point; only one piece of paper is needed. Most people budget and measure each of these flow rates, but they never try to correlate them. The cumulative effect of deviations from these separate budgets cannot be seen clearly and quickly for fast corrective action. One piece of paper is mandatory to show how the bathtub is performing.

Once these numbers have been generated, it's time to assign responsibility. We need to put a monkey on three people's backs for control of inventory. The first is the purchasing manager, theoretically the incorrect person to have a monkey on his or her back, but in practice the right one. Purchasing people rarely make inventory replenishment decisions; they simply execute instructions from others. This is more true in manufacturing than in the distribution or the retail world. The theoretically correct place for the controls is on the people who requisition things for the purchasing department to buy. But such control usually fails because there are far more requisitioners than there are purchasing people, they are more concerned about keeping inventories high than low, and they don't control vendors. Purchasing people do control vendors. So the monkey has to be on the purchasing manager's back for practical reasons even though placing it there is theoretically incorrect.

And what is the allocated responsibility? The purchasing manager has to control the inflow of the purchases at standard cost so it matches the rate calculated by the inventory input-output chart; no more, no less. You should consider this similar to a capital appropriations authorization. Top management authorizes the purchasing manager to spend a certain amount of money to support the business. There is no attempt to control the detailed decisions that make up the monthly numbers; only the totals are controlled. Purchasing people must now work with the requisitioners on the details to ensure they match the totals.

The manufacturing manager gets the second monkey. His or her job is to generate the standard labor value defined by the input-output chart: again no more, no less. This is unusual. Although there is a planned operating rate in the annual budget, it is rarely treated as a budget to be actually met. In some companies there is pressure to exceed the planned rate because surpassing the annual budget will absorb more overhead and show a profit. How you can generate profits by making something but not selling it beats me, but that is what some financial systems calculate. The pressure is always to overproduce. But where does this overproduction go? You guessed it: right into inventory. And since more purchased materials have been consumed by this production, more materials are now ordered. Manufacturing people magnify the inventory investment when they work more hours than budgeted, because of the greater proportion of material in a product's cost.

And the last person with a monkey is the sales manager. He or she has to be held responsible for the outflow of shipments from the plant or distribution center. Agreed, getting shipments out is not always the problem of the sales manager alone. If the company manufactures or assembles to order and the products have not been made on time, there is little that the sales manager can do. But in a make-to-stock environment or in a make-to-order plant with reasonably reliable delivery performance, the sales manager is the key person. Therefore, the sales manager *must* be held responsible for flowing product to customers.

And now we have three budgets and three people responsible for their respective numbers. All that remains is to measure the actual flow rates continuously and aggressively. Significant deviations must be countered with a recovery program to get back on budget quickly. It's this constant unrelenting pressure on the totals that will get inventories stabilized and at the level the corporation can afford. It will also stop the amplifier effect of inventories, at least from this link in the manufacturing or distribution chain to the next level upstream. As we cannot hope to control the economy in total, maybe it isn't bad for a start to simply prevent inventory amplification from the units under our control.

Beware of the cop-outs that will be formulated by all three managers with monkeys on their backs. They will try to get you focusing on details; the totals will then become useless. Don't let it happen! There is no question that details are important, but only after the totals are in balance, not before.

Here are some of the cop-outs you'll hear:

"I don't control the marketplace. Customers either buy or don't buy. How can I be responsible for ensuring a rate of flow out of the plant? The best I can do is simply measure it and that's it."

As soon as you agree with this statement, you are saying that the outflow cannot be controlled with a valve but that the valve must be replaced with a flowmeter. This means that the two other flows—purchases and direct labor—must be more aggressively managed. I have no problem with this, although I am confident that outflows can be managed more than many salespeople will accept. The problem with this statement is that it makes the input-output chart dynamic; hence purchases and direct labor must be varied more often. Juggling vendors and operating rates of your business could become costly. A better solution could be more control of the outflow with sales promotions, price discounting or firming, and creative financing arrangements with your customers.

"I don't control what I buy. I buy what I am asked to. Put the monkey on the back of the requisitioners."

As mentioned earlier, this is the theoretically correct thing to do, but in practice it's wrong. Put the monkey on the back of the purchasing manager. It's the only place where it really works.

"I need to work overtime this weekend to get that big shipment out. You know it's the end of the month and we haven't yet met our shipping budget. I've got to use overtime to do it."

This is an enticing trap, isn't it. We are at the end of the month, shipments are below plan so far, and a little overtime could spring a large shipment. But what if you have generated the labor component of inventory for this month already? Working overtime will book more labor dollars into inventory and drag in some materials. If the shipments this month don't exceed plan, you have just authorized a very expensive buildup in inventory, paying premium for overtime. The real question is, "Why weren't the hours generated earlier in the month spent on this big order so it would be ready to ship without overtime?" They must have been spent on something not needed, more ineffective capacity, for instance, for this condition to occur.

Another key point is that most inventory changes happen slowly, not quickly. Increases are the result of a lot of little decisions being made in favor of "more," not because of one or two big decisions. Working overtime is one of these little decisions, as is subcontracting some urgent work, or ordering a little more a little sooner. You have to keep a lid on these decisions. The only way is aggressive management of the totals.

It should also be clear that some of these numbers could be tested before they become reality. This is obviously the way to control inventory and prevent wrong actions from occurring. This could be called preventive inventory management, that is, "Don't let it occur," rather than defensive inventory management: "Worry about the excess after we have it." The latter is our normal operating mode. A time-phased picture of the standard value of outstanding purchase orders could show you whether next month's commitments to vendors match your budgeted inflow. This information should be easily obtained from your purchase-order system. If the two factors do not match, action can be taken *now* to correct the situation instead of simply recording what happened after the fact. The purchase-commitment report should be a key management number, indicating how much cash is committed to vendors; it is also a good measure of how far the lead-time syndrome has progressed. But it is rarely even known, let alone used as a control item. As the commitment increases, the purchase-commitment report could be easily related to the planned output rate of the company to see if the commitments are reasonable. If the commitment period is lengthening or is increasing faster than planned output, then the lead-time syndrome is in its growth stage. This early warning should focus even more attention on flow rates from suppliers to prevent the wrong items from being ordered and, inevitably, the simultaneous increase in inventories and shortages. Similarly, the order book of a make-to-order company could be compared with the shipments budget. If they didn't match, sales programs could be implemented to make them closer or the budgeted inflows changed sooner to minimize disruption with vendors and the plant. An extending order book is also an early warning that the lead-time syndrome is at work, so extra caution is required.

The historical ratio of labor inflows to inventory can be compared with future plans for operating rates. A simple ratio should help predict whether these operating plans meet the budget, and if not it can provide time to adjust them.

This look-ahead comparison of planned actions with the budgeted totals will be explored more in Chapter 9. It is obviously an integral part of a well-controlled inventory planning and control system.

Subsets of the total input-output chart can be made for segments of inventory. These subsets can sometimes provide more control because they focus on specific areas and break the total inventory bathtub into smaller ones. Figure 6-2 shows a variety of these small bathtubs. Input-output charts can be made and data measured for each of them, provided the financial system generates the necessary data.

But real control comes from the overall chart. Don't let this greater detail take your eye off the totals. It is only control of the total flow that gives you control of inventory.

Balance the Flows

One of the primary reasons for oscillating inventories is flow rates that are out of balance. Purchased materials flowing proportionally faster than direct labor is nothing but trouble, and nothing but inventory. And this is not unusual. Capacity increases (direct-labor additions or more machines and tooling) usually lag any pickup in business. Purchases, on the other hand, especially of standard products, can be increased very quickly. So an out-of-balance condition occurs easily.

A company that I once visited in Los Angeles had this problem but didn't know it. I visited them at the request of the general manager, recently promoted from being the chief engineer. (Can't we pick 'em? Exactly what training does a chief engineer have in running a total manufacturing business? And that goes for the sales manager, financial director, and manufacturing manager too. The answer: nothing! And we wonder why decisions are made that harm our businesses and disrupt our economy.) His problem was that orders from customers were on the increase, but he wasn't shipping. Customer deliveries were bad, complaints were rising, and he wasn't sure what to do.

My obvious answer was, "You have a capacity problem." He said, "No way! I asked the manufacturing engineers and factory supervision, and they said they had all kinds of capacity. The problem is purchasing; they have too many shortages." I said, "In that case you have a vendor capacity problem." He said, "No way! I've asked the purchasing people and they told me if they ever brought in all the stuff that is currently past due—we wouldn't know where to put it. They said the problem is manufacturing doesn't know what they want. They keep changing their minds about what they want to work on next. So we just expedite the needed things as soon as they tell us. Maybe the problem is, I have too many customer orders." (How about that for a nice logical conclusion?)

Here is the typical infighting between purchasing and man-ufacturing seen in many companies. Each blames the other for failure, and no one can sort out who is right.

I said, "Do you have an inventory input-output chart I can see?" He said, "What's that?" So I described it to him. We checked around and the answer was no. I said, "We are going to develop one right now and get to the bottom of this quickly. Tell me at cost of goods sold or inventory-relief dollars how much you would like to ship each month." He said, "$4 million." I said, "Let's go and see your chief financial officer." The general manager said, "Why the financial officer? What's a financial officer know about capacities and vendors?" I said, "More than manufacturing and purchasing in this plant."

The chief financial officer provided the information shown in Figure 7-2 by answering these simple questions.

Question: What is the mix of material and labor at standard costs in the cost of goods sold, and how variable is the mix over time?

Answer: It averages 60 percent material and 40 percent labor and factory overhead, and has been remarkably stable for almost 30 years.

This allowed us to calculate the desired flow of dollars per month through these two streams: simply 60 percent of $4 million and 40 percent of $4 million.

Question: How much have the dollar flows been on average over the last 3 months, and how stable have they been?

Accounts payable provided the material receipts information, remarkably close to expected. It was also fairly constant over the past 3 months. Labor distribution gave us the labor inputs, and they were also fairly stable over the past 3 months. The shortfall was obvious; capacity was the major problem.

Required to ship $4 million cost of goods sold per month

Category	Historical ratio, %	Desired flow	Actual flow (av. last 3 months)	Negative deviation, %
Material	60	$2,400,000	$2,355,000	< 1.9 >
Direct labor	40	$1,600,000	$1,470,000	< 8.1 >

Fig. 7-2 Financial capacity data.

We then went to see the manufacturing people with the data. Their reaction was, "We are working on the output of department 106. It's the bottleneck area. We have some new tooling coming in that will increase output there by 20 percent. As soon as it's working we will have excess capacity."

Some comments are in order. First, there is rarely one department or area of a plant that is so badly out of balance with the next that if you increase production in one significantly, all your problems go away. As a result of intuitive decisions, work centers are fairly evenly balanced. Solve one bottleneck and the next one is immediately apparent.

Second, most hard-goods plants are not machine constrained, they are people constrained. That was certainly true in the Los Angeles plant. Increasing the efficiency of one small area would not have solved the overall personnel problem.

Third, there is a "lean and mean" syndrome at work in most manufacturing plants, meaning that management people think that if they keep the direct labor a little low, the labor will be more efficient. This is a bunch of hogwash. Low direct labor creates an inefficient plant because of the shortages inadequate capacity causes, the excessive overtime needed to generate shipments, especially at the end of the month, and the high inventories, since purchased parts flow into the plant at a higher rate than labor consumes them. A lean and mean plant means high stocks, poor customer service, high costs, and hence low return on investment.

Thirty years ago or more, labor was such a high percentage of a factory's costs that the lean and mean philosophy was probably a good one. Today the direct-labor portion of our costs is so low as to be almost insignificant. Hence a "fat and on-schedule" syndrome would be more appropriate, meaning enough labor to guarantee that the flow rates for the business are in balance. This is particularly important where shipments are concerned. If low direct labor stops the flow rate out of the bathtub, it's obvious what will happen to the level; inventories will increase. And at today's interest rates this will cost more than a little additional labor.

Now you can't take this too far, of course. Labor needs materials to work on. If you have too much labor, you generate excess inventories of finished goods or work in process. But enough labor or a little excess will almost always be preferable to a little less.

Returning to my Los Angeles plant example, it is easy to calculate how many direct-labor people they were short. They had on the payroll 500 direct-labor people working 20 percent overtime on the average. This resulted in a shortfall of around 8 percent. Assuming that the 20 percent overtime figure was acceptable and efficient (a bad assumption in most cases because of the increased absenteeism, poorer quality, and tiredness this causes) and that additional people would be as productive as the existing people (another bad assumption because as a factory expands its labor force, labor efficiency usually drops), then 40 extra people were required. If they wanted to cut the overtime drastically and allow for the drop in efficiency, then at least 100 people would be required. When I suggested this latter figure, reaction from the manufacturing people was *panic*! "Where do I put all these people, what skills do I need, how will I absorb them, and where will the materials come from? We already have shortages with just the existing people. If you add another 100 the shortages will get worse!"

But you and I know from the flow-rate figures that the majority of the shortages were manufactured parts. Oh yes, there were some purchased-part and raw-material shortages, but not many. And part of the reason for these latter shortages was that the manufacturing department kept changing their schedules to work around the other shortages, or to work on the latest hot customer's order, so the purchasing department had no clear idea of what was needed when. Vendors were only expedited from the latest shortage list that the manufacturing department generated from their most recent schedule, instead of expediting based on the vendor commitment date.

The conclusion to the story is that a hiring and subcontracting program was started. It was carefully done so that subcontract receipts were classified and booked through the accounting system as material and labor at standard cost. One month later, shipments started to increase and inventories decreased. The input-output chart from that moment on has been the general manager's favorite control tool. He rides the three contributors to ensure that they meet the flow rates needed to effectively operate the business.

Lest some of you feel I have not considered productivity improvements adequately, let me set your mind at rest. In manufacturing there are some quickly controlled items and others that take time. Productivity is one that usually takes time to improve. The Los Angeles plant was in significant trouble and needed help quickly. So additional labor inputs were quickly made. If significant productivity gains had been possible and had been achieved, the recorded labor distribution would still have shown the improvement because it always records labor at standard cost. If you have a shortfall in labor and you decide to attack it through a well-defined productivity improvement program, the labor distribution report will still be your scorecard. You have to generate standard hours or standard dollars to make a product.

It's worthwhile to discuss again the balance of inventory between labor and material and the mix of flows coming into inventory. The tendency in manufacturing is always to be biased toward higher purchased contents in inventory than in labor. The lean and mean syndrome as well as the reticence in manufacturing to increase capacity without a corresponding reticence to buy materials and parts guarantees it. This means that high inventories in a plant don't necessarily mean an ability to deliver products to a customer. In the Los Angeles example, the general manager was making noises about reducing the past-due backlog by shipping out of inventory. But he didn't have a high finished-goods inventory; the majority was in work in process. If the work-in-process inventory had been balanced, this would have been an excellent suggestion. But it wasn't, as the historical flow rates told you. So here was the dilemma: high stocks going up even higher but customer service deteriorating and shipments stable or dropping. The bathtub runneth over.

The mix of labor and material in inventory is critical. It must be in balance. Flow rates must be adjusted to guarantee a balance. Inventory then becomes a usable commodity instead of a wasteful drag on business health.

Operating versus Financial
Assessments

This section should probably be entitled "Keeping Score or
Playing the Game?" But as that would probably offend the
accountants of the world, I've used another title.

It is true that our traditional financial assessments of business
performance do not encourage better operating performance,
especially where inventories are concerned. Let's look at some
ways of measuring success—I will pick the most blatantly
wrong ones—to see if I can prove this point.

Purchasing is first. The only real financial scorecard of a
purchasing department, besides their operating budget, is
"purchased-price variance," defined as the difference between
what was actually paid for something and its standard cost.
We do not consider how much is purchased versus the
budgeted inflow; neither do we give penalty points if parts
are received early or late. Can you imagine a measuring system
that gave a pat on the back to the purchasing department
because they bought something at less than the standard cost,
regardless of whether it was received when needed or not?
That is your classic accounting system at work. What does
receiving purchased materials early or late cost you? Inventory!
If the materials are early, it's obvious. If late, then all the other
things you received or made on time cannot be put together,
so inventories appear again. On top of this you have all the
other costs of factory disruption and possibly poor customer
service to add in. And don't forget that shortages trigger the
"more" philosophy, sure to end up as even more inventory.

Let's look at the manufacturing department next. The primary measurement of this group, from floor supervisors all
the way up to the vice president of operations, is productivity.
This is evaluated through two measurements, efficiency and
labor utilization (indirect-direct ratios), which are calculated as
follows:

$$\text{Efficiency} = \frac{\text{standard hours generated}}{\text{actual hours booked on direct labor}}$$

$$\text{Labor utilization} = \frac{\text{actual hours booked on direct labor}}{\text{actual payroll hours}}$$

Both figures are usually expressed as a percentage, for example 87 percent efficient, 90 percent labor utilization.

Don't forget: these are the primary measurements all the way through the manufacturing organization. There is enormous pressure to make these numbers higher. Imagine that you are a supervisor on the factory floor. You get praise or criticism based on these two primary measurements. There are several jobs in your area you *could* work on. Which one will you choose?

Any supervisor who survives chooses a job that is either the easiest, hence one where the highest efficiency is generated, or the one with the least amount of indirect work such as setup. She is also tempted to run more than the required lot size any time she can. The extra pieces are always the most efficient because of the learning-curve effects or yield improvements, and she generates more direct-labor hours and fewer indirect hours if she doesn't have to make another setup. All the supervisors in some plants have the same middle name: "Overrun." So Jane "Overrun" Smith makes a few extra any time she can, and she gets a better scorecard from the system and no penalty for the extra inventory. That's someone else's problem. I'll leave you to figure out what happens when we promote our best supervisor, the one with the highest efficiency and best indirect-direct ratio, to production superintendent, then manufacturing manager, then vice president of operations.

It's even worse than this. Because she runs the "gravy" jobs whenever she can, the needed parts are late. So she gets to run overtime to make up the shortages, and her people all get a fatter paycheck. They think she's a great person, and she is to them. But how's she doing for the company? She's the company's worst enemy, building up inventories using premium time.

What about the sales department? The primary measurement of this department is the value of orders booked compared with the budget. If they sell more than budgeted, they are in great shape. If it's less, they are in trouble.

But what if they're selling things we don't have and not selling things we do have? Does their scorecard extend to mix? Have you ever seen a sales manager in trouble for selling more than the forecast but a mix different from the forecast? No way. Such a manager is a hero. But how about that inventory. Selling things not planned for or not in stock triggers additional procurement and manufacturing. It's obvious this will end up as additional inventory. But whose problem is this? Rarely the sales manager's.

So a series of operating measurements that takes precedence over our traditional series of financial measurements is required to manage inventories. For the purchasing, manufacturing, and sales departments, the primary scorecard must be the input-output chart. Are they flowing products at the rate needed to support the inventory budget? The secondary measurement has to be mix. Are they buying, making, and selling the right things at the right time? Only after these functions are being executed well should the traditional financial measurements come into play. Their job is now to value good inventory performance.

The emphasis has to be on optimizing the business, not optimizing functions within the business. "Optimized subtotals" means a suboptimized total, as shown by the earlier discussion of performance measurements. An "optimized total" may mean suboptimized subtotals. A set of optimized business measurements, one of which is inventory performance, is required first. It would be better for the business if the manufacturing department made enough of the right things at the right time a little inefficiently than if it did not make enough or made the wrong things at the right time efficiently.

This suggests that all investors in and lenders to manufacturing or distribution businesses, as well as corporate officers of multiplant companies, should insist on getting reports on all of these operational measurements along with the traditional financial reports. As a minimum, you should get the input-output chart to guarantee that flow rates are in balance and that money is not being spent needlessly. An even better way of showing the interrelations of the various flows of product is to use a graph like that of Figure 7-3, which plots the annual expected shipments at cost of goods sold, purchases, and labor value at standard cost, all on a cumulative basis. The graph also shows inventories. Actual figures can then

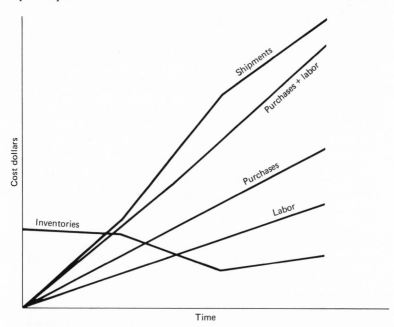

Fig. 7-3   Inventory input-output chart.

show where significant deviations from budgeted values are
occurring and what results these are having on inventories.
Corrective actions should be easily apparent. The cash the
business frees using this approach can then be used productively or effectively to really enhance the business.

Manage the Outside Factories

It is clear that a company's success is heavily dependent on
the performance of its customers and vendors. Company
decisions are based on the flow of information from these two
sources. Earlier chapters have shown how this information
flow can be very misleading because of inventory amplifications
of real business changes. So a primary defensive measure
against false information and wrong decisions has to involve

managing the outside factories. This suggests additional roles for the sales and purchasing departments of a business. We'll look at them in turn and propose what these additional roles should be.

Salespeople must get volume-demand data from customers. This must be real demand, not influenced by fictitious inventory changes. This means talking to the right people in the customer's facility. This will rarely be the purchasing people, as their information has already been processed through the inventory system; hence it is subject to question. The top managers in the customer's company are the best source for quality data, and of course many vendors have these meetings for this very reason.

Beware of false information coming even from this source. Depending on where your customer is in the logistics chain, the information could be good or bad. The customer could be severely influenced by the inventory decisions of several other levels of manufacture and distribution.

You might even consider adding a specialist in inventory systems to the sales department or giving the department support from the factory's inventory specialists when needed. A visit from this specialist to your customer's inventory specialists could pay off tremendously with more valid demand information. Such a visit could certainly remove some of the bias from every salesperson's report of the potential market figures.

This information should now be converted into a contract defining the rate of flow from your plant to the customer. Lead times for the specific items that make up this flow should be very short. In the majority of cases the time necessary to make any item in a factory is just a small fraction of the quoted lead times. If capacity has been reserved and materials are available, it is possible to make almost any item very quickly.

Let's go back to the lead-time syndrome described in Chapter 2. Imagine that the vendor had a flow-rate contract with one customer for one order per week, with the lead time to define specifics of the order maintained at 3 weeks. It would be a most boring time for the vendor, who would receive one order per week as regular as clockwork. The standard lead time of

3 weeks would always apply. Since forecast inaccuracy would be prevented at the customer's plant, the vendor would not be badgered with changes to the orders. One order per week would always be received, exactly what the vendor wanted, and the right things would be shipped exactly on time. Some people would say, "What a dull place to work!" But what a profitable place to work.

The sales department's job is first to sell the capacity of the factory, and second to take short-term specific orders that make up this capacity. As soon as they accept these roles, you have largely insulated yourself from the inventory amplification cycle.

The job of the purchasing department is to convert the permissible overall flow rates, as defined by the input-output chart, into flow rates from each vendor. These flow rates must then be converted into capacity contracts with the vendors. Specific orders for specific items should be placed short term to fill the reserved capacity. Any attempt by the inventory system to change these flow rates must be attacked immediately as invalid, and inventory amplification prevented.

Again referring to the demonstration of the lead-time syndrome, if one customer had a contract with the vendor for one order per week, with specifics defined 3 weeks out, the game would probably be very boring to this customer. (By the way, the demonstration kit can be played this way to reinforce this point.) The customer would not be affected by the lead-time syndrome except for its influence on the horizon of the capacity contract. As the lead time for specifics would be only 3 weeks, the customer would not be affected by the forecast error as represented by the die. The customer would place an order for a specific each week, receive the right thing at the right time each week, and have a cumulative penalty of zero. This customer would win the game every time. Another dull but profitable place to work.

So the purchasing department's role is to plan and control flow rates into the company and to prevent inventory amplification from passing throughout the system to the vendors. By keeping lead times short, purchasing people will also stop the lead-time syndrome from triggering the "more" syndrome;

they will especially ensure that they are buying the right things and not the wrong things.

But beware of the negative feedback these ideas will generate. A company making electronic components used several lead-time-syndrome demonstration kits to educate their salespeople in the terrible consequences which occur when invalid orders are triggered. The salespeople quickly understood the situation since they had participated in it in the real world. Their comprehension of the reasons was vastly improved, though, through playing the game. But then demand for their products exceeded plant capacity. The only sensible thing to do while waiting for the increased capacity to come on stream was to allocate the current capacity to the sales force, with short lead times for specific items. If not, the lead times would extend quickly, and there you would be once again in trouble. But how do you allocate the product? The company based the allocation on historical percentages. But all the salespeople objected because this effectively froze their earnings. New business, the source of additional commissions, could not be taken because the allocation prevented it. The salesperson in one territory was always trying to get more product, but of course with a limited capacity the only place to get it was from another territory's allocation. Hence this salesperson's earnings could only go up if another salesperson's earnings went down.

Salespeople are competitive, so the discontent in the sales force at the allocation system finally forced the plan to be abandoned. The salespeople immediately started selling more than the capacity could support, lead times escalated, triggering even more orders, and the problems were off and running. The impact on the business was terrible. It was bought by a large company shortly afterward.

The purchasing people will tell you that they are more committed with a flow-rate contract, that they can't shop around for better prices, and that the vendor won't honor this contract as much as a purchase order for specifics. These arguments are all false. You are less, not more, committed with a flow-rate contract. You have infinite flexibility in the specifics you order short range. With a purchase order for specifics long range, you are committed even though you know you are wrong. If I worked in a purchasing department

I wouldn't be able to lick the stamp on the envelope most of the time, I'd be laughing so much. Can you imagine sending a purchase order for a specific item, specific quantity, and specific delivery date beyond about 8 weeks and thinking these forecasts are correct? And then to think you are less committed with this level of detail than simply defining a flow rate with no specifics is ridiculous.

How about shopping around? Well, as soon as you've placed a purchase order, whether it's for a specific item long range or for a flow rate over the same time period, you have stopped shopping around. You are no better or worse off, one way or the other.

Will the vendor honor a flow-rate contract as much as purchase orders for specifics? That depends on your negotiations with the vendor. At least with a flow-rate contract it will be easy to measure whether the flow rate matches what was promised. This is not very easy with specifics because of the changes we introduce as we refine our forecasts and send revisions to the vendors.

There are also some tired business clichés that must be overcome. "An order in your hand is good business practice" is one. It's not if the order is canceled sometime later and not if the order triggers you to make wrong decisions.

"Large backlogs mean a healthy business" is another. They're not healthy if they have been triggered by lead-time escalation, they're not if backlogs are canceled sometime later on, and they're not if backlogs represent fictitious demand.

"Order flows higher than shipments means the economy is booming" is yet another. "Boom" is the right word, but with a meaning different from that intended. "Order flows higher than shipments" means, in the majority of cases, lead-time escalation and false demand, sure to generate an explosive increase in excess and wrong inventories, which are sure to be readjusted in the future.

Capacity Decisions

It is obvious that 90 percent of our capacity additions are made at exactly the wrong time. This was shown in Chapter 5;

ineffective capacity destroys our ability to support real customer needs. As soon as we manage the outside factories, capacity changes can be made at the right time, to suit *real* demand, not fictitious backlogs.

Instead of waiting until "healthy backlogs" indicate the need for more capacity, why not add capacity sufficient to handle projected demand increases? Real market share can then be gained at the expense of those who simply increase lead times.

And why not always have the ability to quickly change your demonstrated flow rate? This can be done through overtime, subcontracting, or temporary hiring and will be cheaper in most cases than excess inventory, the only other alternative.

Make sure any capacity additions are flexible ones. Industry is full of stories of specially built equipment lying idle because the specific items being sold are different from those the machine was designed for. If it takes 2 years from the time equipment is justified until it is in place, and the equipment has an amortization life of 5 years, then 2 to 7 years in the future is the forecast horizon for specifics. This forecast will invariably be bad, so plan for flexibility. You can get fair information about volume needs this far in the future, but specifics will be wrong no matter how hard you try. Plan for this flexibility in your capacity decisions.

Clear Responsibilities

If you want to insulate yourself from the inventory amplification cycle as much as possible and prevent your actions from amplifying changes and adversely affecting your vendors, it is clear what must happen.

You must get as much information as possible from your customers on their real demands in flow-rate terms. The sales department must then sell this rate long term with specifics defined short term.

The manufacturing department must have enough capacity to support the needed flow rates with short lead times for specifics. Capacity additions must be made ahead of time based on real demands, and this should be flexible capacity.

The purchasing department must buy capacity for the long term and order specifics for the short term. They should ensure that vendor capacities are adequate to support your future planned operating rates.

And lastly, top management must insist on the input-output chart as their primary control to guarantee that details correspond to the input-output chart's flow-rate figures. The value of outstanding purchase orders and capacity commitments with vendors must match the purchased inflow budget. The direct-labor work force, overtime, and subcontracting must be sized to suit the direct-labor inflow budget. Sales orders plus the forecasted sales must match the shipment budget. And changes in outstanding purchased commitments and order backlogs must be watched to warn of lead times' changing the real demand picture.

With these responsibilities assigned and measured, inventory amplification and the lead-time syndrome will largely be conquered. Inventories will become a stabilizing force in our businesses and in the economy instead of the amplifiers that they are today. And maybe, just maybe, they will be reduced to levels below anything previously thought possible.

Chapter
Eight
Right
Inventory
Level

Here is a subject crowded with emotion. If you talk to sales and marketing people about how much inventory is needed, the answer is invariably, "More! Don't forget, you can't sell from an empty wagon." The problem with the salespeople's statement is they can't tell you how much more or which items they want. Whoever heard of a good forecast for specifics? They just hope that with more of everything they'll have the right things.

Ask manufacturing people how much inventory is enough, and they will also say, "More." They want more raw materials and purchased parts, especially the ones they might run out of tomorrow. But again they can't tell you which items these will be or how much more they need.

Talk to the designers. They want less of all those things they're going to obsolete tomorrow through engineering changes. But they can't tell you which ones these will be, so their input is not much use either.

The financial people want less to improve cash flow and possibly retire some expensive debt. But they don't know how much less or which items won't be hurt with less. Their contribution is not much better than anyone else's, except they are the only ones putting constant emphasis on less.

Why Have Inventory?

To get us closer to a solution, let us understand why we have any inventory at all. What role does it play in operating a business? Once we determine the reasons for inventory, maybe we can see more clearly how much is needed of which items. The implications of this to a business and then to the total economy will be explored.

The reasons for inventories can be put into five categories as follows:

Lot size: We buy things or make things in batches that exceed our immediate needs.

Fluctuation: Sales and production rates are not always smooth; they vary. Hence safety stock is needed for sales fluctuations and work in process for production fluctuations.

Anticipation: Production or buying must occur earlier than the need at times, for example to support an upcoming sales promotion or vacation shutdown, or as protection against a strike.

Transportation: We need to move products from place to place, either between factories, between distributors, or from one to the other.

Obsolescence: You bought or made too much of this item the last time.

For some of these categories, we have mathematical formulas to decide how much inventory of each item is needed. For others it's judgment, experience, or the lack of control that creates inventory. It should be clear by now how these categories of inventory feed on each other. Procurement lot sizes calculated by the customer become erratic demands on the vendor; hence the vendor calculates that safety stock is

needed to buffer the fluctuations. Lot sizes for the manufacturing department become erratic flows through the factory;
hence higher work in process inventories are required. And
then we have the nerve to call the lot size formulas "economic
order quantities." For whom are they economic?

Safety stocks are increased any time lead times increase.
Lead times increase when work in process increases. So these
three factors are linked together in a logical system, pushing
inventories higher and higher or causing inventories to reduce
when any one of the factors reverses direction.

We can also agree that some of our judgments regarding
inventories, their value, and the protection they give, are
stupid. Safety stock planned in a dependent, nonrandom
environment to cover the triple-forecast error problem when
lead times are 40, 50, or 60 weeks long is ridiculous. How can
we predict today the triple-forecast error potential and decide
what level of safety stock will keep us out of trouble at that
point? It's obviously impossible. But look at your inventories,
talk to the inventory planners and purchasing people, and see
what they are doing. You know what you will find? The longer
the lead times, the more contingency in your system. But is it
the right contingency or enough contingency to cover the
triple-forecast error problem? If it were right you wouldn't
have any shortages, would you? I won't embarrass you by
asking how many and which items are on your shortage list.
I have shown in earlier chapters that inventories, especially
work-in-process inventories, increase whenever increased demands generate more disturbance. When capacities are not
proportionately increased quickly enough, more interrupted
flows are created from shortages; hence work in process
increases to compensate.

We can therefore conclude that almost all inventories are
needed or are created when flow rates are erratic. The only
category of inventory for which this is not true is transportation,
the smallest category in terms of total assets. So if flow rates
were smooth, which means many small lots, then lot-size
inventory would be low; fluctuations in demand would be
low, and hence safety stocks would be low; and work in
process would be low because of the balanced flow rates in

the factory. Figure 8-1 shows this concept clearly. Compare it with Figure 5-6. With flows balanced between all inventory pockets, the levels in the bathtubs can be kept remarkably low.

This means that almost all inventory can be categorized as a large adhesive bandage covering up the problems of business. And this is exactly the opinion the Japanese have of inventory,

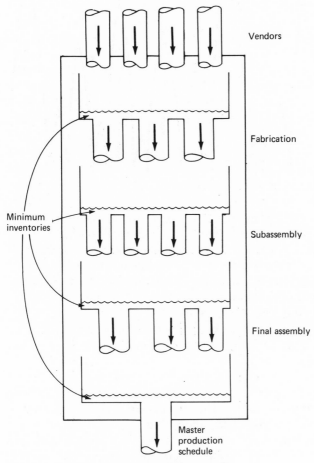

Fig. 8-1 Refinery analogy with low stocks.

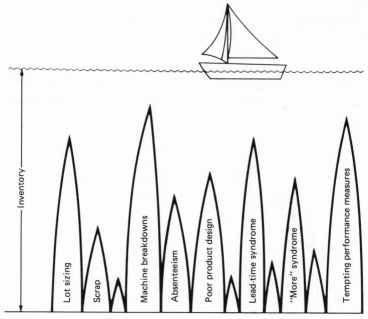

Fig. 8-2 Japanese lake analogy.

that it is evil. They have a wonderful analogy regarding
inventory. They say it is like a lake with rocks on the bottom,
as pictured in Figure 8-2. The rocks represent our failures to
create a smooth flow, because of problems such as lot sizing,
absenteeism, scrap, machine breakdowns, lead-time syndrome, poor performance measures, poor product design, etc.
As long as the lake is full, representing high inventories, the
rocks are covered and the boat sails peacefully along. The cost,
though, is huge inventories and inventory amplification as the
rocks get bigger or smaller.

Now the answer to the question "How much inventory
ought you to have?" is clear. It depends on the height of the
rocks. If as a management team you are prepared to dredge
the rocks out of your lake, then "less" or "a lot less" is the
answer. If not, resign yourself to high inventories and the
associated problems of the wrong inventories. You cannot
drain the lake with large rocks in it; the boat will crash into a
rock and sink.

Involving All Departments

This conclusion has some serious implications for all departments of a business and to some departments that never regard their actions as influencing stock levels. Plant maintenance people must see their job as keeping machines and equipment running. Breakdowns must be fixed quickly. This contrasts with the philosophy in some plants, where the highest priority could be fixing the general manager's toilet! It also contrasts with the idea that maintenance is an overhead and so should be kept very small, and inventories of spare parts to fix broken machines are expensive and should also be kept to a minimum. These philosophies are guaranteed to be paid for with high factory stocks, probably costing more than is saved by squeezing the maintenance activity.

Design and manufacturing engineers must see what their actions do to stock levels. A company I visited had just completed designing a new line of products and was in the early throes of producing the line. It is an electronic product line, so it is based around large printed circuit boards. The product makeup is shown in Figure 8-3. Six different bare boards can be assembled into 22 subassemblies, which in combination with other items make up 56 end products. The lead time from the start of subassembly—beginning to insert

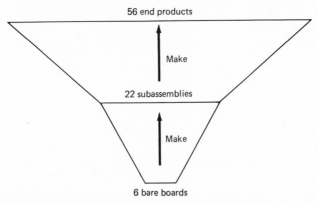

Fig. 8-3 Product makeup.

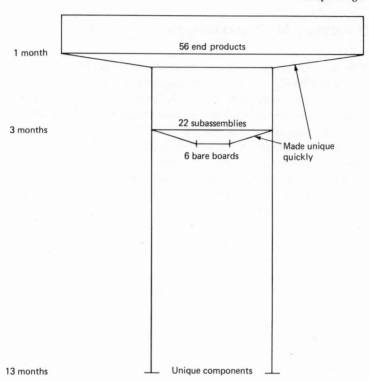

Fig. 8-4 Time-phased product makeup.

components—until the boards are tested and calibrated is 2 months. Final assembly, testing, and packaging takes 1 month. Now the product is ready for the distributors and their lead times.

Guess which operation is performed on the boards first? You're right: pins insertion, which makes each board immediately suitable for only one of the 22 finished boards. So someone has to predict how many of each of the 22 boards should be made 3 months before delivery to the distributors. And this for a new product line, the toughest forecasting problem there is. Add to this the distribution lead time and you can see that the triple-forecast error problem is significant.

To compound the problem, several of the unique components

needed to make the 6 bare boards into 22 finished boards have long procurement lead times, up to 10 months in the worst case. So now the procurement decisions for these components, based on the stacked lead time, are made on a 13-month forecast plus distribution time for 22 specific items. I'll leave you to figure out the triple-forecast error problem potential and whether safety stocks will cover it. This environment is shown in Figure 8-4.

A better approach would have been as in Figure 8-5. The 6 bare boards should have been assembled with their common components first. The unique components should have been left till last. If it was not possible to reduce the 10-month lead

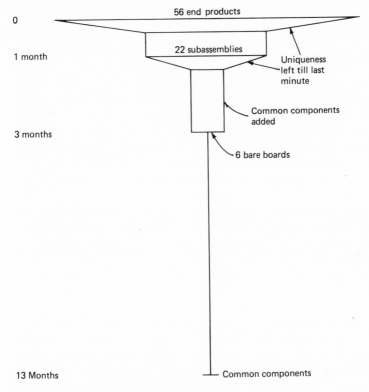

Fig. 8-5 Preferable product design.

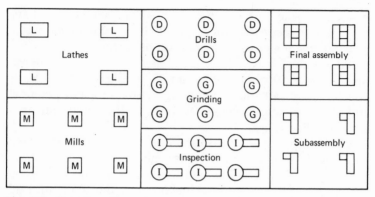

Fig. 8-6 Functional layout.

time for components by contracting for capacity, then the long-lead-time items should have been common to the 6 boards, not unique to the 22. I realize this is not always possible, but I also know that designers and manufacturing engineers rarely consider lead times and the triple-forecast error problem. Their primary emphasis is on function and cost, not on planning, scheduling, and the resulting inventories.

In the example company, production was seriously hampered because of shortages. Manufacturing variances were high and there was enormous pressure for more. Inventories were already high for this product line and were still growing. The distributors were upset because they couldn't get enough of the specific end items that were selling and because they were overstocked on those that weren't. So the emphasis on function and direct costs was misplaced. Some additional direct costs to get more of the right things at the right time would have really paid off, and the design was later changed in order to do this. The design and manufacturing engineers' rocks were reduced and inventories immediately dropped.

The same attack must be made on quality control, accounting, and all the other functions of a business. They all contribute to high stocks, and so must be enlisted to help reduce the stocks. If these problem areas create a rock, then stocks will be high. As they remove rocks or make them smaller, then stocks can reduce.

A different approach must be taken in our factories. Too many of them have functional layouts, with all similar machines grouped together, as shown in Figure 8-6. Products flow erratically between functional areas as they are processed, creating fluctuating demands. High work in process is inevitable to cover the variable demands on the work centers.

Processing layouts, in other words making the factory look like a refinery, can improve this situation remarkably. An example is shown in Figure 8-7. Here similar products flow along a line of machines. The input is raw materials; the output is a finished item. This approach puts a double hit on inventories. The items flowing down the line are all similar, and, if things are scheduled properly, the machines can be set up much more quickly than with the erratic flows of the functional layout. So lot sizes are reduced. The space allowed between each processing step is kept small, forcing inventories to be low, so the line must be capacity balanced. The result of these two hits on inventory can reduce inventory to a small fraction of what a functional layout dictates. It may require more capital equipment to operate this way, but this is a productive asset traded off for that nonproductive asset, inventory.

This concept that the physical layout of a plant contributes to high or low stocks is not understood well enough. There is a law about inventories, caused because of the "more" syndrome, that "inventories will always increase to fill the space

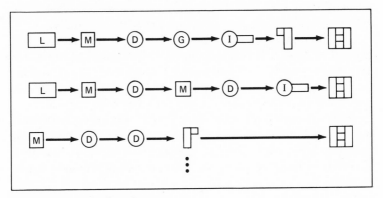

Fig. 8-7 Process flow layout.

available." Now this may be a bit facetious, but don't forget that the processing layout prohibits high work in process. Also, don't forget those industries that manage inventories the best. They are either those with high volumes that can't store much inventory, those for whom the physical space requirements are prohibitive, or those with a process flow. So it's not as facetious as it sounds. Receiving docks, inspection areas, stockrooms, and warehouses will all benefit from a space evaluation. If you think you have too much stock in any of these areas, cut down the space allocation by physical means. The stock will drop automatically; it has to.

So the answer to the question "How much inventory should we have?" has to be "less." Inventory reduction should be used as the means to expose the problems (the rocks) that are hurting the business. Careful dredging of each rock will enable the business to operate better at the same time that stocks are reduced again to expose another problem.

Inventory Is an Asset

This comment may seem to be a little obvious, but it isn't. An asset has to earn a return. But how much is your inventory asset earning you? More than it's costing? In the majority of cases the answer is no. It's costing more than it's earning. In that case, your inventory is not an asset, it's a liability.

You must evaluate all inventories to see if they are earning a good return on their investment. If they are, keep them. If not, reduce them. For example, what if I said, "I can reduce your work-in-process inventory by $1 million, but the probable result will be 5000 standard hours per year of idle time because uneven flows will not then be covered." Another conceptual way of looking at this is, you have to hire three direct-labor people who don't lift a finger all year long in order to reduce inventories by $1 million. Should you reduce the inventories or not?

The answer obviously depends on what you do with the $1

million freed up from stocks and what three direct-labor people cost you out of pocket. Assuming you can invest the money to earn 15 percent per annum or retire debt that is costing this much, that is $150,000 annual income or savings. Three people would probably cost about $30,000 each out of pocket for a total of $90,000 annually. I know what I would do!

This same attack must be made on other inventories, such as lot sizes. The formulas for calculating lot sizes do not consider return on investment. They also have some funny numbers in them that are not the truly variable costs in the decision. If I have a setup worker on the payroll who is not fully utilized, and a machine that only runs 5 hours per day, what is the cost of making one more setup on this machine? I think it is zero. In that case the economic lot size is one. But your company's chart of accounts will not have the same opinion about the costs of the setup. The costs will probably contain the setup worker's time, extended by the hourly rate, plus the machine time at its hourly rate. Hence the economic lot size will be high, creating uneven flows through the factory and demanding even more inventories to cushion the flows. This additional inventory is *not* considered by the lot size formulas but is very real nonetheless.

The return on investment approach should be used to put even more pressure on dredging the rocks. Instead of amortizing the lengthy setups in a factory by building large lots, why not attack the length of the setup and hence reduce its cost? If you can do this, then the shorter setup time can be amortized by smaller lots and lower inventories. This means a smoother flow and thus even less adhesive bandage inventories.

This idea of improving changeover times has not been pushed aggressively enough in manufacturing. We spend a lot of time improving the run times per piece once the machine is operating but do not give equal attention to reducing the changeover times. But the business would probably generate a higher return on investment with slightly longer running times per piece and much shorter changeover times. We would need smaller inventories, and flows would be smoother. These have to translate into increased return on investment.

Now I am sure some of you are thinking that this is not possible, that changeover times are ordained from on high. This is just not true. The technology exists today and is being employed by a few businesses to slash traditional changeover times. Some figures I read recently:

A General Motors plant takes 6 to 8 hours to change over a 600-ton press. Hence they run a 20-day supply of all items.

Volvo can do the same thing routinely in 4 hours. They run a 12- to 14-day supply.

Toyota completes a changeover in 15 minutes. They run whatever is needed, usually no more than 1 day's worth. No, Toyota does not use specially made presses; they are the standard design. Toyota's manufacturing engineers were persuaded of the value of fast changeovers. In conjunction with the floor supervisors, workers, and tool engineers, they engineered setups to be a small fraction of the original times. You now see why all functions contribute to large or small inventories. In this case the manufacturing and tool engineers, with the help and support of the factory personnel, reduced changeover times to reduce lot sizes. That, my friends, is reduced inventories and higher return on investment.

But how about a specially made press if it can reduce changeovers this much? Wouldn't it be worth it? Couldn't you trade off the extra cost of capital equipment against the reduced stocks? A company in Canada has reduced their average changeover times from 3 hours to 1 hour. Their most frequent changeover was 5 hours; it is now 35 minutes. Work-in-process inventories have dropped 32 percent. And this was all accomplished in 6 months. Investments in tooling and other capital equipment to accomplish this change are a tiny fraction of the inventory reduction.

How about the flexibility of the factory with reduced changeover times? With small economic lots and small total inventories, you can make any specific item quickly. You are not subject to forecast error, so you only make things that are needed. Your bathtubs are almost empty, and their content is all good and useful material. Contrast that with filling them with a lot of the wrong stuff because of long changeover times. You see now why the pressure has to be on reducing idle assets and inventories (which are not assets in this case, but liabilities) and replacing them, if necessary, with productive machinery. This revised mix of assets will really pay off by being flexible to changing market conditions. Then real market share can be gained at the expense of the competition.

Ideal Inventory Is Zero

The ideal inventory for a plant or distributor is close to zero. As long as capacity and raw materials are available, any specific item can be made virtually instantly. This may sound ridiculous, but it is being practiced regularly by huge segments of our economy. Fresh food is a good example. Tomatoes, peaches, and lettuce deteriorate quickly once ripe. They must be picked, packaged, and delivered to the end user very fast; otherwise they are garbage. Restaurants exhibit these concepts too. The time between the moment you sit down and the moment you receive a specific meal from a large variety of choices is only about an hour. They have capacity and raw materials. The lead time for any specific is very fast.

We must take this same philosophy and apply it to manufacturing and distribution. Imagine going into a restaurant, ordering a specific meal, and being told, "The lead time on that item is now 4 days, so please come back next Friday!" Ridiculous! But that's what we do in manufacturing and distribution all the time.

The solution involves three concepts:

1. Flow rates must be level, with as few variable or interrupted flows as possible. Buying and selling flow rates will do this for the outside factories. Dredging the rocks out of the lake will solve the problems in the inside factory.
2. Capacity must be applied to a specific at the last possible moment, only when you know exactly what's required. Capacity must be flexible and available when needed.
3. Raw materials or purchased items must flow into your facility at the same rate as you are consuming them, with short lead times to define the specifics.

Practice these three concepts and you will be as accommodating as a restaurant. Listen to the technicians who tell you, "We're unique, we're different; it can't be done with our products" and you will be inflexible to change with huge stocks nobody wants. In other words, you will be a typical manufacturer or distributor.

Chapter
Nine
Role of
Systems

All inventories are managed through a replenishment system using either order points or material requirements planning, as described in Chapter 4.

The key point with both techniques is that replenishment decisions are made item by item. Each item has its own particular available inventory, lead time, safety stock, and order quantity. Even though material requirements planning is triggered by overall plans to make a specific product, and detailed plans list the demands for all items in the product's bill of materials, replenishment decisions are made by inventory planners one item at a time.

Nowhere is there any consideration in these two techniques to the total flow. To make it even worse, the quantity of replenishment, besides the timing of replenishment, is made item by item. What's the chance of all these individual decisions adding up to the right totals? The answer is slim to none. But books, articles, computer programs, and more sophisticated ordering systems are being created all the time, all addressing item-by-item decisions. Little is being said about the totals. What's economic about an economic order quantity (EOQ) calculation if the company goes broke because of the high stocks that EOQs said were economically feasible?

We also know that our attention to specifics creates the inventory amplification problem discussed in earlier chapters.

As we develop more sophisticated systems and mathematics to manage each item, we make the problem worse. The software package described in Chapter 2, put on the market to manage finished goods, is a good case in point. And the situation is even worse than described earlier. Not only does this program automatically update lead times, but it also automatically adjusts safety stocks and lot sizes. The orders thus triggered will place increased and erratic demands on the supply network, causing the suppliers to increase safety stocks and amplify their vendors' demands even more. What has been achieved? We have finally computerized the lead-time syndrome and the inventory variables so that boom-and-bust cycles will occur even faster and with a greater amplification.

The great hope of all management people was that computerized inventory replenishment systems would reduce inventories as a percentage of sales. Actual experience is that they have not; if anything they have increased them.

Look at the inventory-sales ratios published by the U.S. Department of Commerce shown in Figure 9-1. For manufacturing and trade in total, the ratios are steadily going up, meaning that inventories are a higher percentage of monthly shipments. For manufacturing only, there is more variability, but there is certainly no marked improvement; if anything there is a slight deterioration.

I can't say too many times, the problem is that the sum of thousands of details will never add up to the right totals. You only have the right inventory level when the flows in and out of the bathtub are balanced to give you the right inventory level.

Category	Year										
	1971	1972	1973	1974	1975	1976	1977	1978	1979	1980	(July) 1981
Manufacturing and trade	1.62	1.50	1.55	1.75	1.64	1.64	1.61	1.61	1.68	1.68	1.70
Manufacturing only	1.90	1.75	1.80	2.1	1.95	1.86	1.88	1.80	1.92	1.98	1.98

Fig. 9-1 Inventory-sales ratios. (From U.S. Department of Commerce.)

This suggests, no, demands that the details in our systems must become subservient to the totals. We must exercise top-down control, not bottom-up control. It is imperative that we take this approach, not only to overpower the illogical logical system, but also to overcome the emotional decisions that are applied to items one at a time. Don't forget the Johnny Carson syndrome described earlier.

The idea of using top-down control instead of bottom-up control is rarely used in industry. Large retail stores do a much better job than most industries because buyers are also responsible for inventories within a predetermined budget. When stocks in the stores reach this level, no more buying is allowed. The inventories must be reduced before additional buying can occur. If they bought the wrong stuff, then promotions and price reductions are used to move this merchandise. And these cost or price reductions show up in the profitability contribution reports submitted by buyers.

But this approach is rarely used by other industries. Decisions to buy or make something are based on an assessment of need by a system, completely unrelated to budgeted inflows.

The one exception is fair shares distribution, described earlier. Contrast this with the normal "pull" system used by almost everyone else, both distributors and manufacturers. With the "pull" system, decisions regarding inventory needs are made at each stocking point with complete disregard to the total impacts. Inventory amplification is the result.

System Changes

It is obvious that using systems which manage details is the wrong approach. We have to modify this philosophy if we want to make real progress where inventories are concerned.

The starting point has to be the inventory budget and associated input-output chart. This sets the foundation for all detailed, item-by-item decisions. The next step is to force the system to add up all its planned detailed decisions to see if they match this total. This is very easy with material requirements planning and the time-phased order point. It is not so easy with the standard order-point or two-bin system.

But the first two techniques, assuming they are followed perfectly, provide a forward look in quantity terms at the planned ordering decisions and the resultant inventory. Tables 4-1 and 4-2 show these quantity-oriented techniques. Look first at the purchased component in Table 4-1 and the time-phased order point of Table 4-2. If this time-phased order point is being used by a distributor, then it is also for a purchased component. Therefore "released factory orders" becomes "released purchase orders," and "new production needed" becomes "new purchases needed."

All inventory systems have a cost value assigned to purchased items. It becomes a simple process, then, to extend the quantities of "released purchase orders" and "new purchases needed" by the inventory value of each item. This shows the dollar inflow projected for this item. Adding all items together will provide a picture of the total purchased inflow planned for the future.

For the manufactured parts we already know the labor value of items we produce. If we now convert the time-phased order point example of Table 4-2 back to a manufactured part and look at the manufactured parts in Table 4-1, it is easy to see how to value the projected labor inflow. If manufacturing lead times are long, it may be necessary to prorate the labor over the lead time to get a clearer picture of flow rates. Adding together all projected labor inflows by item will provide a picture of the total projected labor flow. The sales forecasts, order book, or production schedules in the system can be converted into dollar outflows in a similar way.

Calculations can also be made of projected inventory levels based on this plan. "Released factory orders," "new production needed," and "planned start" can be converted to work-in-process inventory values. "Free stock on hand" plus "safety stock" plus "new production or purchases needed" will give projected stockroom or warehouse inventories. Now the question is, "Do the projected inventory levels match the budgeted figures as set by the input-output chart?" If not, something has to give. And don't forget, the system assumes perfection in executing the plan, which is sure not to happen. You *will* have late and early deliveries; customers *will* buy a different mix than that forecasted; scrap *will* occur in the factory. All these deviations from the plan will cause a need for more inflows and higher stocks. So when making the comparison, allow for this deviation.

But now, how do we get the right figures from the input-output chart to change the wrong details in the system? We need some way of forcing the right totals onto the details. This process must also smooth out the peaks and valleys caused by the system parameters of lot sizes, etc., which are now clearly seen. And it must force inventories to cushion, not amplify, changes in demand.

Because of the large number of items in most inventory systems, Pareto analysis is the only logical way to attempt to do this. In most distributions, and this certainly applies to inventories, there are a few items, called the "significant few," that contribute a large amount to the distribution, and a large number of others, called the "trivial many," that contribute very little. Hence, when calculating the planned inventories and flow rates, the system must also provide a list of the significant flow-rate and inventory items. For example, the purchased parts making up the planned purchasing inflow in the next few months could be listed in descending order of their contribution to the total, a typical ABC analysis. A similar picture could be made of the manufactured inflow. Attacking the biggest contributors will most quickly show maximum results. The changes that can be made are very few. Either lot sizes, safety stocks, or lead times of these items have to reduce. A program to do this must be started so it is both controlled and realistic.

As soon as the feasible changes are determined and put into action, the system can be updated and the resultant inventories and flow rates can be recalculated. This will prove if the program was successful or not and if further work is required.

It is obvious that this line of reasoning will lead you to its ultimate conclusion: very low stocks. Lot sizes will be small except in a few cases. Production will consist only of the things that are needed short term. Safety stocks will be eliminated except where flow rates cannot be made smooth. Lead times, hence work in process, will be slashed. And the average factory or distributor will need only a small percentage of the original inventories to operate profitably.

The system's details should also provide knowledge of the stacked lead times for all products. This is so easy to do with the information we have in our current state-of-the-art systems.

All manufacturers have ways of retrieving information about their bills of materials from their computer systems. One way to do this is the "indented bill of materials." In the classic case, this means printing the part number, quantity, or some other data element for each ingredient in a bill of materials to show its structural position in the product makeup. For example, major assemblies could be indented one character position, subassemblies two positions, components three, and raw materials four. A slight modification is to add a time scale to the report. The indenting is then not a set number of characters but rather is the lead time for this particular item. A clear picture of the stacked lead time for products results, as shown in Figure 9-2.

An aggressive campaign can now attack those items with maximum payback. A major assembly with a long lead time means all its components are being purchased or made much earlier than the customer-need date, creating a high risk of the

Weeks 0 1 2 3 4 5 6 7 8 9 10 11 12 13 14 15 16 17 18 19 20 21 22 23 24 25

```
    1200—Pencil
       3151—Cap Assembly
          5874—Barrel
             4785—TUBING————*
             2151—Lock————*
             3826—Insert—————*
             4285—Clip———*
       3440—Body
                   7404—TUBING————*
       5615—Refill Assembly————*
```

Fig. 9-2   Time-indented bill of material.

wrong inventories. Long lead times for unique parts, especially the expensive ones, also means high risk where inventory is concerned. Action plans to change these lead times can now be started based on this clear visibility.

In Chapter 5, I asked you whether you would be willing to invest money 24 months before payout, considering the high risk of a poor-to-zero payout or a payout later than 24 months. I doubt any of you were eager to do so. But this is exactly what happens when the purchasing department places a purchase order for things that won't be shipped for several months. A 24-month interval may be extreme, but check your own figures to evaluate your own risk.

If you produce only make-to-customer-order items, you probably think your risk is quite low. But the triple-forecast error problem is almost as bad in your industry as it is in a make-to-stock or assemble-to-order business. It's the engineers who change the design and the customers who change their specifications that create the forecast error, but you are buying the wrong stuff nonetheless. The problem is that you give the engineers and customers too much time to change their minds. If you could have made the product quickly, it would have been produced and shipped before the changes occurred.

In either case, when stacked lead times are long, you are committing yourself to an investment well ahead of its conversion into a return. It is doubtful that the returns are extraordinarily high, but the risk is tremendous.

The length of the stacked lead times for your products must become a key operating measurement for your business. Any tendency for these lead times to lengthen must be questioned and stopped. Only reductions should be allowed and worked for.

Specifics versus Flow Rates

Our emphasis has been and continues to be focused on the specific items. We try to do the right things with all the different items and assume or hope that the cumulative impact of all these decisions adds up to the right totals. It never will.

We have to change our focus to rates of flow. Details must be subservient to the totals. And it's important that we get the details right before they are implemented. You can only control inventory before you have it. Afterward all you can do is bemoan the fact that the inventory is yours.

We also go a long way around to get the information about totals needed to run our businesses. What about the following idea? Start out with an aggregate operating rate for your business, either expressed in financial terms, rates by product family, or tons, feet, etc. In technical jargon we call this the "production plan." Now convert this aggregate plan into specific products you hope customers will buy, called a "master production schedule." Work this plan through the product's bills of materials and create scheduling and buying output for thousands of parts and assemblies. I hope that you are thinking about the accuracy of these detailed outputs and how inventory variables can adversely affect the accuracy.

You must now tell your vendors what you need. They want specifics short term and aggregates (capacity) long term. How can you provide this? Well it's easy: you either place purchase orders long term for all the specific things you need or send them your detailed material requirements planning outputs for all the items you buy from them. Let them figure out what all these details mean to their own capacity. And you'll send them a new report every week and change the purchase order details as needed to really keep them up to date on your latest revised plans. What do you think the vendors do with all this paper every week? What would *you* do with it if you were they. Look again at Figure 6-5 to see how vendors use orders.

This process is completely illogical. We start out with aggregate totals for the business—our production plan—which are bound to be the most accurate numbers we can predict. We then convert them into thousands of details so that our vendors can later add them up again. Do you honestly believe they are then the right totals with all the error, fudging, and mathematics present? I don't. Why go from totals to details and then back to totals again? I suggested doing precisely that earlier in this chapter, that is, costing out the detailed inventory system to see if it matches the desired totals. My only excuse is that most companies have these detailed systems and it was an easy way to have you start thinking about totals.

But why not work from totals to totals, with the details left to the last minute? Wouldn't this make more sense? This means developing systems that convert our aggregate production plan into total flow rates for both vendors and our factory. We have these systems in some plants using the technique called "resource planning," but it's amazing how much emphasis is placed, even in these systems, on details. And the resource plans rarely extend to vendors, although it would be just as easy to use them with vendors as in the plant, with a probably even greater payback.

Once we have the aggregate flow rates, contracts spelling out these flow rates can be made with vendors in tons, molds, units by product family, or any other suitable measure. This is what Bill, the general manager of the casting foundry described in Chapter 6, wanted and couldn't get. Specifics can now be ordered at the last minute and forced to add up to the more accurate aggregate flow rates. And this is when we need our detailed systems, not sooner.

Our performance measurements must also change. We have too many measurements of detail and not enough measurements of the aggregates. Input-output control has to become our primary control tool. All details, whether planned or actual, must be compared with this overall control. Deviations must be attacked aggressively to get back on plan. This means a focus on inventories by all departments to see where improvements can be made.

The assumptions in our systems and techniques must be challenged. The diseases must be cured instead of covering up the symptoms. The analogy of the rocks in the lake should give you plenty of ideas of where to look.

Shop-floor control is a classic case of overkill in most plants. Because of the high work-in-process inventories, supervisors and schedulers are not sure what job to work on next. And because of all the disruptions, today's schedule is of no use tomorrow, so the plan must be revised daily. A huge amount of data from the factory is required to keep track of what items are where in order to generate these revised plans.

But what if every work center had only one job awaiting processing? What kind of a decision process would be left? The choice: either run it or don't. No information would be needed to help the supervisors or schedulers; the choice would be clear. But to get to this ultimate condition requires either smooth flow rates through the plant or a flexible work force to move to busy work centers when needed. This is a much better solution for the business than to have larger and larger systems manipulating more and more details.

The problem is inventory in all forms. We must keep saying inventory is evil; hence less is better. The only reason you need an inventory management system is because you have inventories. The more inventory you have, the bigger and more complex the system becomes. The less inventory you have, the smaller and simpler the system needs to be. So constant unrelenting pressure on less inventory must be the emphasis. Our systems must show the projected inventories and flow rates and provide enough details so that we can change them to the right levels. Only then will inventory and scheduling systems start to pay off with all the benefits that we have been promised.

If we could influence enough businesses to adopt this mode of operating, we would level out the peaks and valleys currently experienced as the boom-and-bust cycle. This would put us on the path to an era of unprecedented growth and stability, and would result in real improvement in both our standard and our quality of living, objectives which are well worth striving for.

Chapter Ten

Inventories and Their Mismanagement

Far too many people feel that inventory is a valuable asset. "It's like money in the bank," is a common expression. This philosophy is especially prevalent when inflation is high. Large inventories purchased or made earlier means that they were purchased or made at less cost.

But inventory is not like money in the bank. Money can always be spent, used to purchase productive machinery or invested in high-yield securities. Inventory must be sold before it's the same as cash. And if it's the wrong stuff, it's about as far removed from money in the bank as it can be.

Inventory management has an enormous influence on our economy. It has a whiplash effect through the logistics chain, amplifying small real-demand changes into enormous boom-and-bust cycles affecting raw-material producers. It is not just the increase and decrease in inventories that is of concern. It's what our inventory systems do to order flow rates and backlogs. Actual inventory changes in industry are relatively small compared with a year's production. It's the effect of increasing and decreasing lead times on order flow rates that makes business leaders feel positive or negative about the economy. These feelings of confidence or concern about the future are translated into decisions about expansion and contraction which are completely unrelated to real demand. This is the major impact of poor inventory management.

Imports, which increase during the boom times, are tough to shut off during the bust phase of the cycle. Jobs are lost to overseas competitors, our balance of payments goes negative, and hence our country's growth rate is slowed.

Interest rates increase quickly during boom times because of the huge demands for credit to finance inventories and the capital spending boom that is based on false demand. High interest rates eventually squeeze out the consumer, who starts to liquidate debt, so real demand diminishes. The bust cycle starts. Interest rates fail to fall as quickly as they rose because government budget deficits grow to support the increased unemployment.

Every business that has inventory is adversely affected by these fluctuations. When business is booming and inventories are growing, the company's cash is eaten up quickly to pay for the increased stocks. Debt financing is needed to supplement the company's cash flow to pay for the inventory growth and other assets.

Capacity increases are triggered by the fictitious growth in demand, creating even more demands for cash that must be financed. But business is "good," so we think we can afford the debt. As soon as the cycle reverses, the debt load becomes unbearable, and we then have to borrow to pay off the interest costs and the normal expenses of the business. Profits are eroded at the time they're needed most.

Our approach to inventory management is all wrong. The theory we build into our systems will invariably create boom-and-bust cycles and hurt our business performance, not improve it. Our perception that by correctly calculating and managing the details of all parts of our inventory we will get the right total is blatantly wrong. But that is today's methodology.

Emotional reactions toward inventories are also wrong. When an item is in short supply, the normal reaction is to order more sooner to get enough. Johnny Carson's comment about toilet paper is a classic case. Another example is carrying more gasoline in your car's fuel tank or storing cans of fuel in your garage when the supply is short. Neither of these reactions solves the problem; both aggravate it.

"High inventories" means the wrong inventories. The forecast error applicable to all the specific items held in stock guarantees this to be the case. But most of our theory ignores this fact. Nowhere in the mathematics of lot sizing is forecast error considered. The demand for each item is assumed to be known accurately over whatever period the lot size will last. What a ridiculous idea!

So our systems and techniques get us to buy or make many of the wrong things. We either dispose of them by classifying them as obsolete, having a fire sale, or carrying them at huge costs, hoping they will sell eventually. We create idle assets, not productive ones, every time we do this.

Inventories should be considered liabilities, not assets, as they are referred to by our accountants.

Almost all our inventory systems, teaching, and techniques are wrong. Few people have the right approach. We deal in details hoping for the right total instead of the other way round. We don't see that the simple answer to the great bathtub mystery is input-output control, a mechanism to force the total flow level in the direction you want it: down.

Inventories, The Economy, and You

What can one person do to counteract these problems? A huge amount. No, you can't solve the problems of the economy singlehandedly, but you can partially insulate your company from the effects of poor inventory management and stop amplifying *your* demand changes on *your* supply chain.

The first step is to convert from a detailed item-by-item orientation to a total flow-rate approach. Understand the inventory bathtub and get the total flow rates where you want them. Force the details to match the totals. Don't allow small increases in demand to cause large increases in inflows. Get clear information about real demand, as unpolluted as possible by the inventory oscillations of your customers. Set manufacturing or selling rates, represented by the bathtub outflow, to these real demand rates.

The second step is to understand the real reasons for inventory. As shown earlier, we use inventory to cover up our failures. Very little inventory would be needed to run the business if other failures were reduced. So an aggressive attack must be mounted on failures, the rocks in the lake. This will take a commitment from the company and the allocation of some resources, but the payback will be worth it.

Take the rock labeled "shortages," for instance. The primary reason for shortages is that long lead times trigger the triple-forecast error problem. How do you reduce your lead times? It's simple. First, reduce inventory. Second, sell to the manufacturing people and salespeople the fact that reducing stocks will reduce shortages and increasing them will make it worse. This is exactly contrary to accepted "common sense" and amounts almost to heresy. But that *is* the solution, done carefully, of course.

Third, attack the traditional measurements of inventory. These invariably aggravate the inventory oscillation. Days of supply, inventory turns, and return on investment are all dangerous measurements as long as inventories are high. Force inventories to become so low that they cease to be a significant part of a company's investment. Hence inventories will not be leveraged to meet return-on-investment objectives as the economy fluctuates. You should also calculate what your company's financial information says your inventories cost. Some plants and divisions of a few large corporations have done these calculations, and they found annual implied inventory carrying costs as low as 3 percent. It will always be difficult to get a plant manager to reduce inventories with such a low charge when productivity and absorption of overheads have a much larger impact on the financial results. The manager's approach will be to have lots of stock in order to be very efficient. It doesn't matter if there is too much, slow-moving, high-risk inventory if there is such a low-cost penalty to the manager's scorecard.

Fourth, increase your emphasis on capacities; decrease it on specifics. Work to make flow rates quickly responsive to change. This will require a new way of thinking at all levels, especially in the manufacturing and financial worlds, but it is a necessary change nonetheless. It could cause you to have idle excess machinery a fair proportion of the time. But what is inventory except idle assets? Your decisions on labor power, cross training of your workers for flexibility, and the use of overtime and subcontracting should all be carefully thought through to provide this responsiveness to changing flow rates.

Fifth, resist committing resources to a specific item until the last possible moment. Keep the resources of capacity and material flexible. When you really know what's needed, make the product quickly. Don't make the wrong thing too soon in the search for productivity. This will only give you the lowest-cost obsolete inventory in the world. Don't let a drop in interest rates persuade you to rush out and buy or make inventory. The thoughts "Inventory is cheap insurance, and we'll use it sometime anyhow," or "With high inflation, inventories are a good hedge against cost increases" have to be tempered with the realization of the triple-forecast error problem. Evaluate this for your business before loosening the purse strings on inventories.

Do these things and you will make a huge contribution to your company and a small one to your country's economy. I can't think of a better use of your time, can you?

A Changed World

The days of cheap and abundant raw materials are gone. The less developed countries, the major source of raw materials, are using their increased political muscle to exert pressure to get a larger share of the world's wealth; the Organization of Petroleum Exporting Countries (OPEC) is an extreme example of this changed state of affairs.

This means that traditional thinking about inventories must change. We need huge amounts of capital to invest in alternative sources of raw materials. For example, off-shore oil wells and oil shale development must be explored to reduce our dependency on unstable foreign sources. But since a large proportion of our capital is already tied up in inventories, it is frozen as far as further investment is concerned. We have idle assets instead of productive ones.

Huge amounts of these idle assets can be freed quickly if we understand how to manage inventory.

Time is running out for us. Other nations are approaching our productivity and will pass us soon. The manufacturing productivity of Japan passed that of the United States in 1967, not a well-known fact. It is estimated that by 1985 the overall productivity of three or four countries will be superior to ours. This is a scary prediction that has significant implications for our way of life. But we can confound these pundits if we choose. It's just a matter of choice.

A Change in Thinking

There's an enormous education job ahead. Our thinking about inventories and their replenishment is all wrong. Economists and business editors must see the link between order flows, lead times, backlogs, and real demand. The economy is *not* healthy when order flows exceed shipments, and sick when they are below. People are simply tinkering with lead times and the inventory variables. Real demand is not changing very much, even though order backlogs held by durable-goods manufacturers oscillate wildly. We must find a way to discount the lead-time syndrome and changing inventory variables when reporting the health of our economy.

Our use of increasing and decreasing vendor lead times, order backlogs, and inventories in our economic performance indicators is highly questionable. But what to use for a substitute? Inventory-sales ratios are not much better, because one company records a sale as another records an increase in inventory. This ratio fails to show the true state of inventory amplification.

Maybe the only measure that makes sense is the actual change in inventories. We know these fluctuate plus or minus

10 percent when real demand only changes plus or minus 2 percent. Anytime inventories increase faster than end-consumer demand it should be clear that false demand changes are occurring. This should be cause for concern rather than a suggestion that boom times are coming. Don't forget that a boom for this reason must be followed by destocking and a bust.

Bank managers and investors must view inventories as a black hole consuming critical cash. Inventories are not necessarily assets just because that's where they appear on the balance sheet. We must learn to question order backlogs and see the reasons behind them. A large, healthy backlog is a contradiction in terms. How much strength do you place on a company's large backlog when making loans or investment decisions? Don't ever forget that every order placed is three forecasts, all wrong to some degree. But even more important, don't forget that every order placed can also be canceled. And there goes your large, healthy backlog.

Investment decisions must be made on the inherent strength of the business. How competitive is the business? What's the balance sheet look like? Are inventories a high or low portion of assets? And so forth. Most business ratios do not separate cash from inventories, assuming they are both current assets. I think I have shown the fallacy of this thinking.

Sales personnel, purchasing agents, manufacturing people, schedulers, planners, systems people, and above all, top management need a different outlook. The top-down instead of the bottom-up philosophy must prevail.

It's interesting to reflect how much training we give people in how to manage 50 percent of a company's assets, its inventories, and 75 percent of its cost of goods sold. These are average figures, showing how much these areas are affected by the inventory management of manufacturers; the figures are probably even higher for distributors and retailers. The answer is that we give pitifully little training. And as I have said numerous times, I am not just concerned with the people responsible for materials management, purchasing, production, and inventory control. I mean the people in all departments, because they all affect inventories, as shown in Chapter 8. We give far more training to people with far less direct influence on the business, such as data processing people, than we do to people contributing to the success or failure of inventory management. Correct this imbalance, and you'll get some short-term tangible payback.

We also need to evaluate our traditional organization structures. You will often find the control of inventories fragmented among a variety of departments. The production control people report to the production superintendent. Inventory planners report to the vice president of operations. The warehousing and distribution people report to the sales manager. And the purchasing people report to the accounting people, believe it or not. How can you possibly get a coordinated attack on inventories with this diffused responsibility?

Even when these functions are centralized, as in a classical materials management organization, the materials manager usually reports to the manufacturing manager or vice president of manufacturing. It is obvious that this relationship emphasizes the manufacturing concerns. As we have seen, the manufacturing department's task is to produce, but production usually ends up as inventory.

A few companies showed remarkable improvements in their inventory performance after materials responsibilities were centralized and that manager reported to the general manager of the operating unit. Trade-offs between the various departments and their specific objectives can then be made with a higher degree of attention to inventories throughout the business. The rocks in the lake can come from many areas, for example, industrial relations, quality control, and design engineering. If the responsibility for inventories is buried in the organization or fragmented among areas, it is impossible to generate enough drive to attack inventory levels. With responsibility centralized and elevated to a high enough level, inventories get the attention and management they deserve.

Chapter
Eleven
Inventories
and the
Economy

I have alluded several times to the devastating impact of inventory and lead-time decisions on our economy. I will now prove this statement by using examples from the *Wall Street Journal* and *Business Week*. The examples occurred during the last major boom-and-bust cycle, 1974 to 1975. Subsequent economic cycles have been much smaller for a variety of reasons. The next major one will be in 1986 to 1987 and will occur for the same reasons as the cycle in 1974 to 1975.

Feast to Famine[1]

Cancellations of Orders Are Starting to Plague Almost Every Industry
Sudden Shift from Shortage Causes Spending Cuts and Spreading Layoffs

Finding "Water" in Backlogs

by Bill Hieronymus
Staff Reporter of the *Wall Street Journal*

"It's just by the grace of God, not good management, that we didn't expand," says James H. Manecke, chairman and president of Ranco Inc.

[1] Bill Hieronymus, "Feast to Famine," *Wall Street Journal*, Dec. 12, 1974.

With a sigh of relief, Mr. Manecke recalls that only a few months ago Ranco was plotting major capital expansions to boost output of its industrial control devices at most of its 10 locations around the world. The bulging order books of the Columbus, Ohio, company certainly seemed to dictate such expansions.

But now, as suddenly as the wind can shift from south to north, Ranco's forecast has changed. Instead of a flood of incoming orders, Ranco is facing some order cancellations. And scores of customers are notifying Ranco to "hold shipment until further notice," Mr. Manecke says. He is consoled at least by the fact that the costly expansions weren't begun.

Here you see the devastating influence of lead times at work. They forced order books to bulge, so expansion plans were in the works. But here is one time slow management decisions were helpful. The business didn't expand, luckily, because then the bulge of orders disappeared fast. You can see the lack of correlation between real demand, backlogs, and order flows in this example.

The article goes on to say that the nationwide slowdown in orders was 3.6 percent in September and 0.9 percent in October, according to the Commerce Department. How's that for a magnifier effect? A reduction in orders of a few percentage points caused backlogs to collapse. The article also stated that hundreds of employees were being laid off in many other companies until orders strengthened again. And all these moves were completely unrelated to the real-demand supply situation.

How can these huge changes possibly be related to real demand? The economy, therefore end-user consumption, doesn't change this much. How could it!

Delivery Times for Many Goods Take a Sudden Turn for the Best[2]

The change results from suppliers' eagerness to keep their plants running by catering to customers. Deliveries from suppliers, says Levi Strauss & Co. are "the best they've been in quite some

[2] "Delivery Times for Many Goods Take a Sudden Turn for the Best," *Wall Street Journal*, Feb. 27, 1975.

time." Fairchild Camera & Instrument Corp. says it receives "virtually immediate delivery" on parts and chemicals that often took two to three months to arrive a year ago. "We've seen as dramatic a turnaround in a short time as I've ever experienced," says Richard M. Bourgerie, vice president of Bendix Corp. Supplies of aluminum and zinc castings, rubber and plastic components and steel, all hard to come by three or four months ago, are easily obtained, he notes.

Are you ready for the world's record?

Even items with traditionally long lead times loosen up. Georgia Pacific Corp. says orders for large, heavy duty trucks it uses are filled in five months now compared with a year's wait just three months ago.

How could this be? How could truck companies have built an additional 7 months' worth of trucks (12-month wait reduced to 5 months) in only 3 months? Where did the necessary capacity come from to do this? You now know that this is not what happened. Cancellations were responsible for the 7-month difference. Workers were laid off by the truck manufacturers because of shrinking order books, and all their suppliers then followed suit. You might want to go back to Chapter 2 to review the lead-time syndrome charts now that you have read this. The full impact of order flows triggered erroneously because of lead-time changes should start to be clear. Decisions to increase capacity because of large backlogs, as in Ranco's case, are also wrong because the backlogs are simply lead-time induced.

One industry that has undergone remarkable changes in the last 10 to 15 years is the semiconductor industry. It is new, fast-growing, highly competitive, and run by aggressive entrepreneurs. It is also a favorite of newspaper and business magazine reporters because of its newsworthiness.

Business Week published several articles about the semiconductor industry that show exactly what happens in the real world. Excerpts from three of them, published between November 1974 and April 1976, talk about the business level and health of the industry. We will soon see whether their opinions match reality.

Semiconductors Take a
Sudden Plunge[3]

Six months ago, the producers of ICs, transistors, and other solid-state electronic components could not keep up with demand.

Please remember this statement. Later we will evaluate whether it was true. It will also be interesting to figure out how this deduction was reached.

Order backlogs had soared, and delivery times stretched out more than a year on major product lines.

Oh! So backlogs and long lead times are the symptoms they used to deduce that there was a capacity problem. I wonder if there really was a correlation.

Big new plants were springing up in such unlikely locations as Beaverton, Ore., and Orem, Utah.

Two more unlikely locations would be hard to find! So we're going to expand capacity to take care of the huge order backlogs, are we! Sounds logical, doesn't it?

But the picture has suddenly and dramatically changed. Many of the new plants are being left half-finished or unoccupied, company after company is slashing its work force, and the first signs of red ink are showing up. During the third quarter, shipments dropped for the first time since the disastrous recession of 1970.

It's happened before, has it? Yes, and will again, about every 4 years. Won't we ever learn?

A Big Surprise. The rapidly deteriorating marketplace caught nearly everyone by surprise. In a few months the industry's big order backlog was cut by half. Order cancellations and returns have reduced backlogs by $620 million since May, estimates Jon D. Gruber of Robertson, Colman, Siebel & Weisel, a San Francisco investment banker.

Why was it "a big surprise"? It happened just 4 years earlier. All the same symptoms were showing in 1974: huge order

[3] "Semiconductors Take a Sudden Plunge," *Business Week*, Nov. 16, 1974, p. 64.

backlogs, ridiculous lead times, and everyone scrambling for more.

> Says Benjamin M. Rosen of Wall Street's Coleman & Co: "One-quarter of the market—the distributors—suddenly stopped ordering and even started returning products. So far, it has been just an inventory correction, but everyone fears that it could extend into end-demand softness.

What did he mean "just an inventory correction"? Weren't layoffs and half-finished plants bad enough?

You can see the lead-time syndrome and our wonderful computerized inventory systems at work here. The distributors actually felt a slight reduction in demand, very small in aggregate terms, yet their inventory systems multiplied this into a huge adjustment of factory output. I'll leave you to visualize the changes that then occurred in the factories that supplied the semiconductor plants. The semiconductor companies magnified the change through their inventory systems into even larger impacts on their suppliers.

A Sparkling Recovery for Semiconductors[4]

> As quickly as it arrived two years ago, the worst recession in the short but eventful history of the semiconductor industry seems to have ended.

So this one was even worse than 1970, was it? I wonder when the next bad one will be?

> Prices are firming, delivery times are stretching out, and some customers are even beginning to fear a repetition of the capacity crunch that touched off a buying panic in 1973.

Here come the symptoms of trouble again, but the headline reads, "A Sparkling Recovery for Semiconductors." You gotta be kidding.

> "It's Katy bar the door," crows James F. Riley, a former president of two semiconductor companies who now heads industry research at Dataquest Inc. in Menlo Park, Calif. He says that a

[4] "A Sparkling Recovery for Semiconductors," *Business Week*, Apr. 26, 1976, pp. 37–38.

check of the major producers of transistor-transistor logic, the workhorse ICs found in most computers and industrial control systems, shows that delivery lead times have jumped recently from six weeks to as long as eighteen weeks. And for the first time in two years incoming orders are outracing industry shipments by 50% or more.

It's Katy bar the door all right. Huge orders were being triggered because of lead-time changes, and the reaction was that business was picking up. Instead, demand probably increased only a few percentage points, triggering order flow rates 50 percent higher than shipments. It's all part of never-never land.

> Most semiconductor executives, while confirming a big influx of recent orders, hesitate to make public predictions of shortages. "Hopefully we learned something the last time around," says E. Floyd Kvamme, who heads semiconductor operations at National Semiconductor Corp. Adds Intel Corp.'s marketing head, Jack C. Carsten: "The sporadic shortages we're seeing now can be patched up by hiring and training more people and by doing some expediting." He does not expect a widespread industry shortage of capacity for another year.

Did you read that right? He mentioned "a big influx of recent orders." In Chapter 4 I showed how a 3 percent change in end-consumer demand could result in an 81 percent change in short-term factory demand. I doubt that you believed me then, but maybe you do now. My question is: Where were all these extra components going? If they were going to assembly factories, doesn't this mean the assembly plants suddenly increased their capacity, hiring hundreds of extra people to do the work? Did they? Of course not. How could they hire and train the extra hundreds needed so quickly?

> **Signs of Life.** But some distributors and customers do not believe him. "We're already seeing some delays in delivery and some partial shipments," says an official at Computer Automation Inc., a minicomputer maker. "On some parts we're getting lead times of 18 to 20 weeks now, which goes past our ability to forecast."

Here you see the triple-forecast error problem in full stride. We will come back to this statement later. It is probably one of the most perceptive comments in the whole article. Maybe you remember the die in the lead-time demonstration. If you do, you see it now being rolled in the real world.

> And Sidney L. Spiegel, who heads components distribution at Wyle Laboratories, says he no longer believes the semiconductor industry can avoid another shortage situation. "It's a shock that it could happen again so soon," he sighs.
>
> One reason for Spiegel's pessimism is that the current surge of orders is coming mainly from distributors and small electronics companies. "The mainframe computer people haven't even started their buying yet," he says.

So the distributors were back in the news, were they? During the recession they were tagged as the culprits. Then during the recovery, there they were again. To whom were the distributors suddenly selling all these additional components? Or was this the inventory system problem at work again? You decide.

> Welcome as this growing flood of orders is to the semiconductor makers, it could also create problems. For one thing, quickly lengthening lead times could force customers to place multiple orders to be sure of getting the parts they need when they need them. While there is no sign yet of the double and triple ordering that plagued the industry in 1973, small customers already are scrambling to get their orders filled.

Sounds like the Johnny Carson story all over again to me. And what's this about double and triple ordering? That's not fair! How can we keep track of real demand while that's going on?

> To keep their bookings under control, the semiconductor companies are urging their customers to make long-term commitments and to predict their needs more precisely.

Do you get it? Forecast further out more accurately. Sounds rather difficult to me. The following comment indicates what is more likely to be the attitude of the semiconductor business.

> But many purchasing agents balk at these tactics. "A lot of people have spent the last year or two working on new products," says Robert Fisher, purchasing manager for Varian Data Machines, the mini-computer arm of Varian Associates. "It's hard to predict what component usage will be for a new product," he maintains.

Without this kind of information, though, the semiconductor
companies are reluctant to add new capacity. "When your backlog
is made up of 90-day orders," says Fairchild's Duffy, "there are
only so many commitments you are willing to make."

Here was someone looking for a "big healthy backlog" to
support the decision to add capacity. I think I have shown
that for this type of industry "big healthy backlogs" are a
contradiction in terms. Why couldn't he see the problem of
1973 to 1974, when the big backlogs triggered false capacity
additions? If you can't see the problem, read on.

Bottleneck. With longer term orders beginning to roll in now,
the semiconductor companies are starting to equip and staff new
facilities that they left half-finished during the recession. Intel,
for example is finishing a silicon wafer plant near Portland, Ore.
(Beaverton), a move that will almost double its wafer processing
capability. And National Semiconductor, by completing a plant
in Utah (Orem) and adding a building at its California head-
quarters, expects to add 25% or more to its capacity.

Well, here's the result of building plants to satisfy order
backlogs: half-finished plants lying idle for 18 months. What's
the return on investment of a half-finished plant? Please don't
tell me zero. I guess now we are all aware that the neck of the
bottle is always at the top.

But now to the coup de grace. An article in *Business Week*
headed "New Leaders in Semiconductors" displayed the
graph shown in Figure 11-1. The reporter plotted for the years
1973 to 1975 the actual shipments by the semiconductor
companies. As you can see, good steep growth during 1973
and into 1974 was followed by the crash in late 1974 and 1975.
A steep upward growth was projected for 1976, actually a lot
steeper than the good growth in 1973 to 1974.

The reporter also calculated the actual consumption rates of
semiconductors by the companies using them to make, for
example, computers, televisions, cars, watches, and other
electronic equipment. Growth occurred throughout this period.
The rate of growth in 1974 to 1975 was a little less than that
in the preceding periods, but it was growth nonetheless. The
reporter also predicted a return to the growth rate of 1974 and
1975 during 1976.

Let's refer back to two of the articles discussed previously. One stated, "Six months ago [May 1974], the producers of ICs, transistors, and other solid-state electronic components could not keep up with demand"! The other stated, "Prices are firming, delivery times are stretching out, and some customers are even beginning to fear a repetition of the capacity crunch that touched off a buying panic in 1973." But wait a minute. This graph shows shipments about 10 percent above consumption. If you can sell me on the idea that this was a capacity problem, you could sell buggy whips to car drivers! And believe it or not, this was when the semiconductor companies started expanding capacity even more. Why? Lead times were 60 weeks, effective flow rates were therefore low, and inventories and shortages were at record levels, so the pressure was on for more. And "more" was translated into more factories.

Another line read, "As quickly as it arrived two years ago, the worst recession in the short but eventful history of the semiconductor industry seems to have ended"! Recession! Where was the recession? Continual growth occurred through-

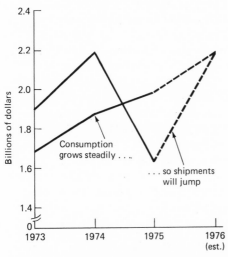

Fig. 11-1 Rebound in semiconductors. (From "New Leaders in Semiconductors," *Business Week*, Mar. 1, 1976. Data based upon *Business Week* estimates.)

out this period, albeit at a slower pace than in 1974 to 1975. But ask the thousands who were laid off in 1974 to 1975 if there was a recession. The answer is a resounding yes. How does this match the lead-time syndrome demonstration game of Chapter 2? Is this proof that the theory works in practice?

Is it obvious that the difference between shipments and consumption is inventory buildup caused by either "logical" inventory systems or emotion to protect against expected shortages? The severe correction depletes inventory for a while (consumption larger than shipments), but it doesn't last long. The fast return to the situation in which shipments are above consumption is a tragic example of the enormous "more" pressure on inventories.

So "a sparkling recovery for semiconductors" was not quite true. In fact it was just the opposite.

More Misconceptions

Business Week contains a regular feature called "Business Outlook." The editors express their views on the economy, explain current changes in business conditions, and make some observations about the future course of business. Let's look at one of these features.

Stockpiling Materials All to the Good[5]

Inventories have been rising faster in the past several months than previously. At the beginning of March, manufacturer's stocks were $124.8 billion—a $6.4-billion increase in a three-month period. Stocks rose only $3.5 billion in the previous three months.

Is it clear that the only way to make stocks increase is to buy or make more than you sell? Here was 1974, supposedly a boom year, with stocks increasing. What did I tell you about the multiplier effect of inventory?

[5] "Stockpiling Materials All to the Good," *Business Week*, Apr. 6, 1974, p. 14.

> The increase, however, is beneficial, not adverse. It is occurring
> largely in materials, not in finished products. And it is occurring
> in those industries enjoying large order backlogs and subject to
> delivery problems.

Now wait a minute. How can building stocks in a boom time
ever be beneficial? The increase was largely in materials, which
means the lower tier of the supply chain was working at a far
higher rate than the demand could support. You know the
inevitable repercussion of this. The only question is when it
will occur. As mentioned earlier, in such cases "boom time"
is probably the best term you can use, but with a meaning
different from the usual one.

> Fully 50% of the advance in stocks since last November was in
> materials and supplies. Work in process soaked up another 26%.
> Finished goods stocks rose only $1.5-billion in the three-month
> period.
> If this keeps up, some of those bottlenecks may begin breaking
> up. After all, total industrial output now is no higher than it was
> late spring. Manufacturers have had a year to work on their
> supply problems.

Let's make sure we understand what a bottleneck is. It is a
resource that has inadequate capacity. A bottleneck cannot
produce more than a certain amount, so it acts as a brake on
business. Thus it holds up all other processes in the business.
But in this case inventories were growing. Didn't we just say
that the only way to increase inventories is to make or buy
more than we sell? How can you do that if there is a bottleneck
resource? The answer is that you can't. So the limiting resources, if there are any, were not creating higher inventories.
It must have been the nonlimiting resources that were generating more.

But of what value are building inventories of some things
while others are in short supply? We need balanced inventories
in factories to make products. Having a lot of some materials
and insufficient of others is nothing short of stupidity. Could
it be that the pressure to increase inventories was causing the
bottlenecks? If this is true, then the whole structure of inventory
management is not only wrong, it is devastating to our
economy.

Here is some more recent history, again from *Business Week*.

Shortages Are Building Again[6]

Nearing the end of the third quarter, many U.S. manufacturing companies face a difficult problem—supplies. Everything from valves and fittings to capacitors, steel castings, and refractories are becoming harder to get. Producers are stretching out delivery schedules and in some cases are putting even old-time customers on allocation.

There go the lead times (delivery schedules) again. What's this about allocation? Didn't they know they should increase capacity to fulfill all these good customers' orders? Or were they still smarting from the terrible financial problems they encountered in 1974 to 1975? Recessions generally follow the pattern of bad, mild, medium, and bad again. After a bad recession we remember the terrible consequences and are hesitant to risk suffering them again. But as time goes by, our memories dim, people retire or are transferred out of key positions, and the management pressure to keep inventories under control diminishes. The "more" syndrome immediately takes over, causing increasingly severe problems until the really bad recession hits. We start the pattern again immediately.

So far there is little evidence of panic buying in anticipation of shortages. Aside from closely monitoring inventory levels, ordering earlier and agreeing to more multi-year contracts, manufacturers are playing the situation cautiously.

As you can see, management pressure was blocking the Johnny Carson syndrome from taking over. But memory has a habit of fading, so. . .

The average lead time on electrical connectors last year was 16 weeks; now it is 32 weeks "and extending weekly," White says. "On bearings that go into jet engines, lead times are going out to 52 weeks from 36 to 42 weeks a year ago," says Harold M. Brodsky, vice-president of operations for the Fafnir Bearing Division of Textron Corp., a major supplier to aircraft, farm equipment, and other industries.

[6] "Shortages Are Building Again," *Business Week*, Sept. 18, 1978, pp. 35–36.

When lead times are extending weekly, you know the lead-time syndrome is at work. There's no way this is a measure of real-demand increases. The silly thing is that it takes no longer to actually make these products when quoted lead times are long or short. It's all a paper tiger that benefits no one.

Lest you think it only happens to industrial products, read the next piece of this article.

> Even such ordinary items as door locks are becoming hard to find. As recently as six months ago, it was possible to buy door locks with a four- to six-week delivery, says Howard C. Bass, sales manager of Forest City-Palevsky Corp., a building supply company in Cleveland. Now the lead time has stretched to 12 to 16 weeks, and prices have increased 12% in the past 18 months.

The link between prices and lead times is a difficult one to prove, but real nonetheless. We'll talk more about this later.

Unfilled Orders Bound Ahead[7]

> The surge of ordering has far outpaced the gains in shipments, which have been registering steady, though less spectacular, increases.
>
> Since last fall, hardgoods shipments have been rising at an annual rate of more than 20%. But the rapid rise in new bookings has maintained a wide gap of more than $5 billion a month between orders and sales.
>
> Unfilled orders of hardgoods manufacturers zoomed $7 billion in January to $237.1 billion. This brings the gain over the past three months to $16.8 billion and puts order backlogs some 26% ahead of a year earlier.

We're probably at week 11 of the lead-time demonstration right now. Everything looks good. Orders are flowing faster than shipments, but shipments are also significantly higher. Profits look good, there's plenty of credit to finance inventories, and don't forget that tight capacity, which is causing some shortages. You know that you have to order more when you are short. And obviously this is going to continue, isn't it?

[7] "Unfilled Orders Bound Ahead," *Business Week*, Mar. 12, 1978.

First Signs of an Inventory Rush[8]

Haunted by memories of the 1974–75 recession, when overbuilt inventories forced them to indulge in an orgy of stock liquidation that slashed profits and prolonged the downtown, businesses in recent years have understandably kept a wary eye on inventory levels. Now a number of economists believe that such caution may be eroding. "We're getting scattered reports from our clients that an inventory scramble is under way," reports Otto Eckstein of Data Resources Inc.

What did I tell you about inventory management being largely affected by emotion. As long as top managers keep the pressure on, inventories are under control. Take this pressure off and look out.

Meanwhile, BUSINESS WEEK interviews with manufacturing executives around the nation indicate that most companies are watching inventories closely. At the same time, however, the executives concede markets are strong, price increases are accelerating, and lead times on orders are widening. As a Westinghouse Electric Corp. purchasing executive puts it: "It's the kind of situation that causes some people to build inventories and to place multiple orders."

Do you recall the semiconductor story of 1974 to 1975? Sounds familiar doesn't it?

Most executives insist, however, that inventory policies remain tight. "People can't afford to hold materials for three months—the interest costs will kill them," says Alvin Glick, president of Alro Steel Corp., a Jackson (Mich.) service center.
Adds Robert C. Parker of International Harvester Co.: "People still carry the scars of having to work off 12 to 18 months' inventory in 1975, so they are being very conservative now."

I wonder how long this will last. One more customer complaint and "thar she blows."

The critical question, of course, is whether this attitude is starting to change. Complaining about stretched-out deliveries of such

[8] "First Signs of an Inventory Rush," *Business Week*, Mar. 26, 1979, pp. 23–24.

items as steel and aluminum, David T. McLaughlin, chairman of Toro Co. in Minnesota, says, "If it gets much worse, we're going to have to start cushioning our stockpiles."

So the hard lessons of 1974 to 1975 are starting to be overridden. The scare of shortages is always more persistent and powerful than the scare of too much. Of course it's an interesting question where the extra materials will come from to "start cushioning our stockpiles" when there is trouble getting the regular supplies. Won't placing more orders for materials make matters worse? Or is he planning to tap another source of capacity, say from overseas?

An Economy with Still No Bottom in Sight[9]

Economists are beginning to talk about recovery, but there is little reason to pay attention to them yet. They know no more than you do about the timing and shape of an economic rebound. The fact is, they cannot even yet figure out how fast and how far the economy will sink and when it will bottom out. How many economists predicted the speed and magnitude of the current decline?

There is only one thing that can cause such a severe and quick change in the economy: inventory. Consumer spending doesn't change that much, maybe 1 to 2 percent in a month. But here's the economy in a steep nosedive with no end in sight.

The Worst Set of Leading Indicators in 32 Years[10]

New orders for consumer goods and materials, in real terms, fell sharply in April—a 15% decline in only two months. And in real terms, contracts and orders for new plant and equipment have been easing off.

[9] "An Economy with Still No Bottom in Sight," *Business Week*, June 16, 1980, p. 57.

[10] "The Worst Set of Leading Indicators in 32 Years," *Business Week*, June 16, 1980, p. 57.

Here is one of the biggest problems to overcome, this watchful eye on new order flow rates. They dropped 15 percent in 2 months. So what! Someone was undoubtedly cutting lead times, so orders automatically stopped being placed. Those wonderful inventory variables—lot sizes and safety stocks— were also being jiggled, causing even fewer orders to be placed. But these don't relate to real demand. And it's real demand that measures the health of the economy, not the size of backlogs or the rate of flow of new orders in comparison to shipments.

The comment in *Business Week* about orders for new plant and equipment easing off is also interesting. It means that the majority of new capacity is added at exactly the wrong time. When backlogs are low, you cannot justify adding capacity. When they are large, you can justify adding the capacity, but it's too late. By the time you get it into operation, the peak of the business cycle is past, so the extra capacity sits idle waiting for the next upturn. You only hope your wonderful, new, shiny capacity will be needed to make the mix of products people want during the next upturn. Stories abound, however, about cases in which this hope was never realized and the new capacity sat idle or was severely underutilized.

No Inventory Problem? Take Another Look[11]

Amid the welter of glum economic statistics this week is one set that is potentially the most damaging of all: the data on inventories.

Economists have been assuring each other that business has been cautious on inventory policy. Warnings of recession, the high cost of carrying stocks, and quick cutbacks in production were believed to have kept stocks in balance.

But in April, stocks of manufacturers rose $4.1 billion, bringing the three-month rise to $10.3 billion. Manufacturers' sales, meanwhile, declined sharply in April, bringing the three-month drop-off to $8 billion.

[11] "No Inventory Problem? Take Another Look," *Business Week*, June 16, 1980, p. 58.

The question is how much control is really exerted over inventories. Maybe they just happen; this is certainly true for many businesses.

> It also brought the inventory-sales ratio to 1.68 from the 1.59 of March and 1.54 of February, exactly where it was before the rug was pulled out from under production in late 1974. In real terms, after adjustment for prices, the ratio is higher than in late 1974. And inventories are unbalanced. Stocks of finished goods are rising faster than goods in process and raw materials.
>
> That spells large cuts in industrial production in coming months.

In earlier chapters I challenged the myth that business really controls inventories. In the huge majority of cases, inventory management is a mathematical process, administered by inventory planners, schedulers, and buyers. There is very little direct influence by the higher levels of management except in a jawboning sense. And quite a lot of these mathematical systems, especially those of distributors and retailers, are driven by past history. They simply extrapolate past sales into the future and plan inventories accordingly. But this means the mathematics lags actual events. How else could inventories grow $10.3 billion at the same time that sales dropped $8 billion? And because of this lag, the crash, when it really does come, will be more severe than the actual drop in demand in order to work off the excess inventory.

Lay-offs Signal a Slump that Will Not End Soon.[12]

> "The electronics industry is in a recession," says Ted D. Gibson, senior economist at Crocker National Bank. Gibson thinks that 5% of California's 400,000 electronics workers could be laid off during the first six months of 1982.

I wonder what the real demand for electronics is? It seems to me, looking at the expanding range of items that use electronics, that real demand must still be increasing. Why are workers

[12] "Lay-offs Signal a Slump that Will Not End Soon," *Business Week*, Nov. 30, 1981, p. 69.

going to be laid off? You guess! Read this account from the
Wall Street Journal.

Construction of Plant Is Halted by National Semiconductor Corp.[13]

The depressed semiconductor business, currently saddled with
excess production capacity, has forced National Semiconductor
Corp. to suspend construction for about a year on a half-built
plant in Arlington, Texas.

Work on the 290,000-square-foot plant, which is designed to
produce five-inch silicon wafers for integrated circuits, was halted
last summer in the midst of a general industrial slowdown.
However, a spokesman confirmed this week that the company
has begun taking down signs at the site "to discourage calls from
subcontractors who want to come and lay down phone cables."
The foundation was poured, and walls erected, before construction ceased.

The spokesman said that the project has been definitively shelved
at least until next September, and probably for a year. "When
we resume work there," he said, "You'll know business has
turned up."

Economic Disruption

Although the previous section might have suggested that I
think the only item affecting the economy is inventory management, I certainly do not think that is true. Interest rates,
government deficits, balance of payments, inflation, population
growth, age distribution, productivity, and a host of other
influences are part of the economic forecasting puzzle. Also
some demand changes, for example, demand for automobiles
and houses, are real. But even these changes are partly a result
of interest rates, caused to some degree by the need to finance
inventories. It's difficult, if not impossible, to sort out the real
changes in demand from fictitious or amplified changes. All I

---

[13] "Construction of Plant is Halted by National Semiconductor Corp.,"
Wall Street Journal, Jan. 13, 1982.

can say is that inventories are a key factor, probably the largest, in causing real-demand changes to be amplified through the economy. They may not trigger the demand changes, but they give them a significant push and become a self-propelling influence.

Let's consider inventory's effect on hours worked. When we experience increased demand, we schedule our factories at a higher rate, and overtime hours are common, so disposable consumer spending increases. More installment debt is taken on because of these "good times." This debt puts demands on the first-tier supply chains, which see this as increased demand (which in truth it really is) and increase procurement to suit. But the first-tier supply chains also increase inventories more (don't forget the theory of inventory management), putting amplified demands on the second tier of supply. This ricochets down the supply chain, getting each level to supply more and build more inventories. More hours are worked, more disposable income is spent, more debt is taken on, and the whole process becomes self-propelling. When the bust occurs, the process reverses itself. Overtime is stopped, layoffs occur, shorter work weeks are scheduled, and so disposable income drops dramatically. Demand drops, inventories are pared, and even more layoffs and shorter hours occur. This continues until a floor is reached; the floor exists because people have to spend a certain amount each month just to live. This money comes either from the wages of those still working, from savings, or from transfer payments such as unemployment insurance or other support programs. With a slight increase in demand or in consumer confidence, the process repeats itself.

The way business looks at these changes and makes decisions regarding investment also contributes to the problem. When business is bad, capacity utilization is poor, so expenditures for new capacity are below the depreciation rate of their existing investments. As business picks up, capacity utilization increases and the company is presumed to be "healthier." Business confidence grows, even though it is a false confidence, and short-term financial performance improves. Sales and marketing people persuade management that "We're gaining market share!" But how everyone gains market share at the same time beats me. This, however, is the prevailing feeling when business booms. Short-term increases in orders are compared with historical rates of sales for the industry. A larger percentage is calculated as increased market share. The fact that historical rates of shipments always lag and are not really comparable to order receipts is bypassed in the glow of success.

As soon as capacity bottlenecks appear, additional capacity is authorized. (A little late, don't you think?) This puts demand on the capital goods sector, which starts to become healthy. Capital goods always lag behind the economy, and now you see why. Capital goods producers put demands on their suppliers, inventories are increased, more hours are worked, and then the consumer goods sector is strengthened, as mentioned earlier. Industrial supplies are linked to both these sectors, so they get a double hit, one when consumer goods production increases and the other when capital goods production takes off. This self-feeding mechanism is what the "supply-side" economists try to stimulate. The terrible danger is the inventory segment, not real demand, that these programs stimulate and the inevitable crash that must result.

Capacity Changes

It's fair to say that 90 percent of all capacity additions are made at exactly the wrong time. When a machine or plant has become overloaded, it is too late to make a decision to expand. But this is what happens in far too many cases. Let's read some more material from *Business Week* to prove it.

The Surge in Capital Goods[14]

Good things are happening in the capital goods sector. According to the Conference Board, capital appropriations of the 1000 largest manufacturers rose to a record $19.2 billion in the fourth quarter, seasonally adjusted—a gain of 17% over the third quarter.

[14] "The Surge in Capital Goods," *Business Week*, Mar. 19, 1979, p. 24.

The fourth-quarter surge boosted backlogs of unspent appropriations by $2.4 billion, to $63.7 billion by year end.

I wonder whether the surge was caused by real demand or simply longer lead times? These jumps seem too much for real-demand increases.

The approval of fatter budgets for capital projects is showing up in order books.

In the three-month period from October to January, backlogs of unfilled orders in nondefense capital goods industries rose by $7.5 billion. After rising at an annual rate of 18% and 16% respectively, in the second and third quarters of 1978, unfilled orders jumped to a 26% growth rate in the fourth.

And given the big increases that occurred in January backlogs may grow just as fast in the current quarter.

This period was just at the crest of the boom time. Here were capacity decisions being made, and significant ones at that, when the growth curve of the business cycle was near the top. Capacity additions take anywhere from 12 months to 3 years to become productive. So these additions were being authorized at exactly the wrong time. By the time they were installed, the decline phase of the business cycle had begun, taking away many of the needs for additional capacity.

Did you notice the rate of growth? Starting at 18 percent, dipping to 16 percent, and then jumping to 26 percent. But this was in unfilled orders or backlog. Do you honestly think this was real demand increasing? Of course not. Our old friend the lead-time syndrome was at work, forcing orders to be placed for long-term future needs.

No Inventory Problems?
Take Another Look[15]

The uniform pattern of the decline of the leading indicators convincingly signals continued rapid economic decline in June and, at least, the early part of the third quarter. What is so worrisome is that there is almost no sign of offsetting gains.

[15] "No Inventory Problems? Take Another Look," *Business Week*, June 16, 1980, p. 58.

Capital spending was supposed to have imparted more residual strength, and inventories were widely thought to be in good shape.

But a collapse in demand of this magnitude should raise considerable doubt about both of these sectors too.

The twin genies, inventories and order books, were at work again. Demand, as measured by order flows or backlogs, was collapsing, causing concern about inventory levels. But inventory levels hadn't changed much yet, it was just the fear they were too high that was causing this trouble.

The outlook for capital goods is darkening rapidly. In April the capital spending survey of the Economics Dept. of McGraw-Hill Publications Co. indicated that business intended to boost spending by 12.2% in 1980.

But now the McGraw-Hill economists anticipate a 9% increase (and a decline of 1% after adjustment for inflation). They note that when the survey was taken "Firms responding to the survey had probably not had time to adjust capital spending plans to meet the changing economic conditions."

You see how capital spending, inventories, and order flow rates work together in synchronization. No wonder we have such vicious cycles in our economy.

This leads to the conclusions that capital spending is expected to weaken considerably in the second half and that "spending in 1981 will rise by 3%, which implies a fall in real terms of 5% to 6%."

So here you see that when the economy is bad, capital spending dries up. But if capital expansions take 12 months to 3 years to complete, wouldn't this have been the time to make them? Or are our personal fears or need for short-term profits controlling logical business decisions?

A Machine Tool Slowdown Signals More Bad News[16]

The Administration's program of accelerated capital recovery is supposed to kick off a new wave of investment. It may take some time.

[16] "A Machine Tool Slowdown Signals More Bad News," *Business Week,* Oct. 12, 1981, p. 40.

Machine tool producers in August continued to feel the effects of high interest rates and low capacity utilization.

Capacity utilization has been low all year and fell in August. And the present cost of capital implies that business must jump the hurdle of very high rates in order to realize a sufficient return on investment.

Why invest in new machines when the old ones aren't running? To beat the competition? Maybe, if you have that much faith in your abilities and in the economy's rebounding sometime soon.

Machine tool orders for the month, as reported by the National Machine Tool Builders Assn., were $214 million—below their year-earlier level for the 13th consecutive month.

Through the first eight months of this year, orders were 35% below last year's total, with shipments outpacing orders by 56%. In August shipments were 72% ahead of orders.

Why the focus on order flow rates? They're clearly important, but we know how much they are affected by lead times. Why can't we measure the real underlying demand?

In August, 1980, an order backlog of $5.5 billion represented a 15-month shipment rate. In August of this year that backlog shrank to $3.9 billion, representing only nine months' sales with no early prospect of a pickup.

Orders are being deferred, and there has been a significant increase in cancellations. Only 12% of gross new orders were canceled in 1980. In July and August the rate averaged about double that.

This article provides more evidence that capital goods spending was drying up. But now I hope you see the lead-time syndrome really at work. Average lead times dropped from 15 to 9 months in 1 year. Order deferrals and cancellations started to appear. Sounds to me like the lead-time syndrome explained in Chapter 2. Six months' worth of orders were deferred or canceled in 1 year because of lead-time changes, and we view this as a terrible slide in the economy. If the lead times had remained constant, there is no question that the bookings would still have slid, but nowhere near as much as this.

And spending was still stopped at the wrong time. Almost all the economic forecasters were predicting a pickup in the economy in the last half of 1982, when demands for capacity would increase. This was then 12 months away, certainly time to start investing in known bottleneck areas, but spending for machine tools was dropping. It was exactly out of phase with logical thought.

Dim Hopes for a Spring Rebound[17]

Hanging Back on Investment. The combination of high inventories, low capacity utilization, and high interest rates has made executives wary of taking advantage of the substantial tax incentives for investment. The depression in autos and housing and the sudden slump in sales across the economy have left them even more uncertain about the outlook.

So we were still holding back on investment even though the prognostications were for an economic upturn. I wonder if we waited too long.

This gloomy assessment of the near-term outlook was reflected both at the American Economic Assn. convention held before the New Year in Washington and in a BUSINESS WEEK survey of company executives. "The economy is much softer than the conventional forecasters are saying," contends Martin Feldstein, a Harvard economist and president of the National Bureau of Economic Research. "The recession will be longer." Adds Richard W. Rahn, chief economist for the U.S. Chamber of Commerce and a leading supply sider: "I foresee an explosion in investment later in 1982, but businessmen are waiting for signs of an upturn in demand before they act."

So there was going to be an explosion in investment, was there? That would mean heavy competition for products from companies that were in no shape to supply. They had laid off many of their workers; they had low raw-material inventories, and they were also low on cash and business confidence. The explosion in investment would be an explosion of placing orders. Backlogs, not investment, would grow. Lead times

[17] "Dim Hopes for a Spring Rebound," *Business Week*, Jan. 11, 1982, p. 34.

would grow, more orders would be triggered, and then we would be off and running. Especially if by then interest rates had dropped enough to cease to be a deterrent.

The whole correlation of capacity and order backlogs is wrong. These two are not linked as many people think. They are only indirectly related.

The load-versus-capacity bathtub of Figure 11-2 should show this clearly. "Load" is the size of the backlog or order book or, in some cases, the size of the pile of work waiting to be processed. "Capacity" is the rate of flow through this facility. In most businesses, decisions are made about the capacity pipes by looking at the depth of water. To prove this is ridiculous, perform the following test.

Send someone into the bathroom with these instructions: "Put some water in the bathtub, as much or as little as you like. Then balance the level of water. Do this by either closing the taps and the drain, or having the taps and drain wide open, or anywhere in between. It is your choice."

After this is completed, go into the bathroom with your eyes closed and ears plugged. Roll one sleeve up and use your arm as a dipstick to feel how deep the water is. Now tell the other person what was done with the taps and drain.

This is obviously impossible. There's no correlation between depth and flow rates. Even when the level in the bathtub is rising or falling, real correlation with demand is difficult because of the lead-time syndrome. It should be obvious that lead time and the depth of water in the bathtub are related.

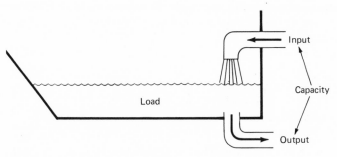

Fig. 11-2 Load versus capacity.

We're looking at the wrong variables when we study backlogs and order flow rates. These variables are not well correlated with real demand. Inventory variables and lead times stop backlogs and order flow rates from telling us about the health of the economy or our business. But economists the world over use these variables to make predictions about the economy or business health. No wonder we have so many wrong projections, even for the next quarter.

Businesspeople use the same variables to measure the health of their businesses. They make decisions about investments in capacity that are largely based on false information. Real demand for a commodity rarely changes that much, but large expansions are triggered because of small changes amplified through the inventory systems of the world, as was shown by the semiconductor story.

Imports

If we could keep the implications of these effects within our own boundaries, the effects wouldn't be so bad. But in today's relatively free trade arena, we have other countries to contend with. There is always product or capacity in some other part of the world just waiting to get a foothold in the U.S. economy. And the truth is, we operate in a way that invites foreign competition into our markets with open arms. We're upset when the foreign competition won't leave and then look for tariff or other governmental protection against this "unfair" competition.

I don't mean that all imports are caused by our failures. Many overseas products have higher quality and performance and are lower in price than domestic versions. It makes sense if we believe in free trade to buy these products offshore. But a large number of imports are begun for no valid reason except our failure to control the elements of inventory and lead time.

Let's look at *Business Week* to prove it again.

Steel's Bright Spot Suddenly Turns Dim[18]

In the opening few months of 1982, one of the few bright spots in an otherwise grim steel industry outlook was supposed to be oil-country goods. Demand for tubing, piping, and casing used in oil and gas exploration was so lively right through the fall of last year that domestic producers, despite a 17% increase in their output, could not meet it. As much as 2.3 million tons of oil-country products were imported by the U.S. in 1981, more than 12% of total steel imports.

So here was the picture: demand was high and domestic capacity had been increased 17 percent, which was still not enough. Imports picked up the slack to the tune of 2.3 million tons.

Prospects, however, are changing. Orders for oil-country goods are falling as the rate of increase in drilling begins to slow and as oil and gas producers start to work off huge equipment inventories amassed last summer. And this is happening just as U.S. manufacturers are starting to add some 1 million tons of new production capacity to the 3.6 million tons they have in operation.

Who said 90 percent capacity was added at exactly the wrong time? Here was a 30 percent capacity increase coming on stream just as demand started dropping.

Oilmen will still probably drill some 400 million ft. of exploratory and production holes this year, or 11% more than last year, calculates Richard L. Head, president of Armco Inc.'s Tubular Div., a major pipe and tubing supplier. But this is substantially less than the 29% increase in footage drilled in 1981 compared with a year earlier. Worse still, orders for oil-country goods probably will not even keep pace with this slower growth and could decline in 1982.

Even though 11 percent more pipe would be put in the ground, plants would ship less pipe. You know the reason: our old friend, inventories!

[18] "Steel's Bright Spot Suddenly Turns Dim," *Business Week*, Jan. 18, 1982, pp. 28–29.

How far they fall will depend on stockpiles held by users and distributors and estimates vary. The purchasing agent of one major oil company sets present supplies at 4.5 million tons of products, or roughly a 9½-month supply. But Peter F. Marcus, a steel analyst with Paine Webber Mitchell Hutchins Inc., thinks they could be as high as 5.7 million tons, nearly five months' more inventory than the oil industry usually carries. "We just know there is a hell of a lot of pipe down here," says Roger E. Bartelsmeyer, vice-president of Cactus Pipe & Supply Co., a Houston distributor.

Why was all this inventory there? Because the Johnny Carson syndrome had been at work. Fears of a shortage of steel tubing caused everyone to buy more. This outstripped the capacity of the domestic suppliers, so foreign imports filled the gap. Not because there was a real supply-and-demand imbalance. Oh yes, there was a small imbalance, but not to the tune of 2.3 million tons per year. But 5 months' more inventory than normal was produced or imported. I'll leave you to calculate how much steel is equivalent to 5 months' more inventory.

Chevron USA, Inc. the domestic oil and gas subsidiary of Standard Oil Co. of California, for example, says its orders for pipe and tubing in the first quarter "are down significantly." As a consequence, producers' shipment estimates are being revised. Armco's Head figures that U.S. shipments this year could be 8% to 12% less than last year, Marcus thinks they will be perhaps 25% less.

The decrease in shipments from the previous year obviously would depend on how aggressively inventory destocking occurred. Since there was surely no shortage of capacity, and demand appeared to be plateauing, the Johnny Carson syndrome would fade away. Let's calculate how much the shipments could drop. Demand was 11 percent higher and stocks were 5 months higher. The increased demand would take about 1½ months' more pipe, so stocks were 3½ months too high. This means shipments could fall almost 30 percent. And this occurred just when a 30 percent increase in capacity came on stream. Oh well, there would always be next year.

The Longer Term.   Imports, too, will probably fall. They could be down as much as 13%, Marcus thinks. But proportionally, he thinks, U.S. manufacturers will bear the brunt of working off the inventory. One of the main reasons is that some buyers, including U.S. Steel Corp. and Armco, signed long-term contracts with foreign manufacturers to ensure adequate supplies for their own customers. They will honor these contracts until they have more capacity on stream themselves in the U.S.

We invited the foreign steel in and got caught in some long-term contracts. Now the foreign businesses retain sales as we lay off the people at the plant. How long can we continue this practice?

In the longer term, some foreign contracts should disappear. "Purchasers don't want to make long-term commitments, and they don't have to if they deal with domestic suppliers" in a more normal supply-and-demand market balance, maintains Armco's Head. In early 1983, more U.S. capacity will be available. And by then much of the current inventory overload could be worked off.

The question is what is a "more normal supply-and-demand balance"? Don't inventories always interfere with the knowledge of real demand and real supply so that we never get a normal balance? I bet we go through this cycle again, and it won't be far off, either. Until we learn to manage the inventory component we will always be its victim.

Meanwhile, however, high-volume commodity grades of U.S.-manufactured piping, casing, and tubing will have a tough time finding markets in the U.S., and prices will probably continue to fall. Already, according to one steel executive, some are being slashed as much as 30%.

What was the logic behind slashing prices? The only value would be if it stimulated additional real demand. But would it be likely that reducing oil-field tubing prices would stimulate well drilling, and enough well drilling would ensue to offset a reduction in prices of 30 percent? I doubt it. Such price slashing would only reduce the speed of destocking and prolong the agony. Wouldn't it have been smarter to hold prices, force destocking quickly, and then return to profitable sales?

This [price slashing] will take its toll on earnings, especially on companies such as U.S. Steel, Jones & Laughlin, Armco, Republic, and Wheeling-Pittsburgh Steel, which depend on oil country goods for a relatively large share of their steel-making profits. Marcus figures that J&L, for example, made 60% of its 1981 pretax profits from the sale of oil-country goods on which margins last year ran as high as 25%. At Republic, about 50% of pretax profits last year came from oil-country goods.

Can you think of a better way to rub salt in a wound? Domestic suppliers increased capacity 17 percent, probably at some cost. They contracted for imported steel, also probably at some cost. They sold a lot of pipe, but a large amount went into inventory. Then destocking dried up orders and prices were slashed, but the imported product kept right on coming. Profits started slipping and the additional 30 percent capacity just then coming on stream sat idle or displaced other capacity. And we are supposed to be in business to increase return on investment, aren't we?

Recession Finally Comes to Oil Services[19]

Prices and sales are also declining for steel pipe used in drilling. A year ago it was in critically short supply, and oil companies, fearing they would get caught short, built up big stocks of pipe.

Did you hear that right? Pipe was in critically short supply, so oil companies built up big stocks of pipe. How can you do that unless the shortage is contrived or fictitious?

They were completing their inventory buildup just as drilling began to slow. New orders have now practically dried up, and steel executives concede it could take the rest of 1982 to work through existing supplies. For the steel industry, this is an exceptionally bitter pill. Oil drilling has been its only lucrative market for the past year and a half, and most forecasters believed it would continue strong this year.

[19] "Recession Finally Comes to Oil Services," *Business Week*, Apr. 26, 1982, p. 127.

You see how inventories cloud information about real demand. Especially when you are removed several tiers in the logistics chain from real demand.

> Now the prospects have changed entirely. Armco Inc. has postponed construction of a $633 million pipe mill. U.S. Steel Corp., while sticking with plans to build a new oil country plant that its customers will finance, is laying off workers in its Ohio and Texas pipe mills.
>
> And Nucorp Energy Inc., a large San Diego-based pipe distributor, is in technical default on $300 million worth of loans and expects to report a significant loss for the first quarter.

Can you see the synergism of inventory building and capacity expansions? As customers start to build stocks, producers think their demand has increased, so they expand capacity. As soon as the inventory bubble bursts, expansion plans are shelved or delayed. So we hit the economy twice on the way up, with inventories and capacity expansion, and twice on the way down, as both are forced into reverse.

Inventories Could Retard the Recovery[20]

> Because of the big declines in energy prices, the bottom has fallen out of the oil drilling industry. "There are currently some 4 million to 5 million tons of oil field pipe on the ground in the U.S., which is about a $1\frac{1}{2}$ years' supply—more than twice what is needed," says Richard L. Head, president of Armco Inc.'s tubular goods division.

So now we're up to 9 months' worth of excess inventory are we? We were up to only about 5 months' worth of excess in January. Some portion of this increase is clearly due to a further reduction in drilling, but how much is due to the reduced prices? And how much is due to those long-term contracts for imports? We'll never know for sure.

This is not simply an isolated example. The same scenario

---

[20] "Inventories Could Retard the Recovery," *Business Week*, Aug. 2, 1982, p. 18.

in a variety of forms can be seen for bearings, castings, semiconductors, machine tools, and material-handling equipment. In some way or other almost every industry has been affected by this terrible circle.

Productivity

Overall, U.S. productivity is still the highest in the world. But our traditional lead over other countries is narrowing fast. It is estimated that West Germany, France, and Japan will all become more productive than the United States by 1985. In terms of manufacturing productivity, Japan passed the United States in 1967! The implications of this to our standard of living and position in the world's economy is nothing short of frightening. Productivity is the engine that allows us all to receive more for less. If we fall from first to fourth place in the world, our whole lifestyle will be threatened.

Inventory management, through its effect on the scheduling of production in manufacturing plants, wastes productivity. It is one of the key areas holding back potentially huge productivity gains; this fact must be recognized and the situation improved quickly.

For a start, let's look at obsolescence. Retired ITT executive Evert Welch said it best: "The only reason you have obsolete inventory is you made or bought too much the last time." This seemingly innocuous statement has significantly more meaning than might appear at first glance.

I haven't found any national statistics on obsolescence, but let me guess it is at least 2 percent of manufacturing production. It doesn't matter whether the products were made efficiently or not. Throwing them away is a loss of productivity in the fullest sense. And to add insult to injury, you probably kept the obsolete inventory on the books for a few years at a significant inventory cost before you threw it away. When I speak of obsolete inventory, I don't mean what you booked as obsolete last year. I mean what's truly obsolete. We all know that manufacturers and distributors decide how much obsolescence to book based on business conditions. But real obsolescence does exist in inventory, whether it is reported or not.

Slow-moving inventory is almost as bad. Such inventories lock up assets, do not earn a valid return, and prevent investment in more productive areas. It would be better in most cases to pay more for the right things at the right time than to have the wrong things bought or made inexpensively.

Why do we have obsolete or slow-moving inventories? By now the Johnny Carson syndrome must be apparent as a key factor. As in the oil-field tubing story, only because of the fear of a true shortage did the 5 months' worth of excess inventory grow to 9 months' worth of excess.

Another factor is the risk of forecast error the further into the future projections are made. The trumpet shape seen in Figure 2-16 shows that when lead times are long, wrong things are being bought or made. Some obsolescence is clearly caused by technological innovation, but I maintain that a very small share of our country's total annual obsolescence bill can be charged to technology changes. And even some of that which can is linked to technology only because inventory systems triggered replenishment of items with a high obsolescence risk.

Another serious factor affecting productivity is the simultaneous existence of shortages and excesses. This is the worst of both worlds. The excess inventories limit investment in productive equipment, and the shortages disrupt the smooth, efficient running of a factory. Go talk to a production supervisor and ask, "How do you spend your time?" The answer invariably will be, "Attending meetings on the latest shortages and their status and physically chasing parts to keep my people busy." Then ask, "How much time is spent on supervising the work force and working with them to be more productive?" The answer to this question will be, "You gotta be kidding. I don't have time for that." But what are supervisors paid for? A large part of their task should be productivity improvements. But the failure of the logistics systems to keep them supplied with the right parts and materials at the right time diverts their attention to simple survival.

Productivity is related to the rate of output of a machine or a resource. Several factors detract from this, among them the time needed to set up the machine, any adverse learning curve effects, and quality problems that can occur early in a batch. Shortages need to be reduced quickly, but many times an efficient lot of product cannot be run. Split lots in order to produce a few critical parts quickly are commonplace, causing the machine or resource to be out of production more often, and generating poorer quality than necessary.

We often add overhead people to cope with this chaos. Expeditors, our favorite professionals, spend the bulk of their time in a crisis mode, worrying about the next few hours of production. They have a job for life, doing enough damage chasing today's shortages to guarantee more problems tomorrow. They thus disturb efficiency in every area they touch.

Ask your purchasing people, "How much time do you spend negotiating with vendors for better materials at better prices with better terms and conditions?" If you're lucky, the answer will be 5 percent. Many times it's even less than that. Instead they are processing change orders to the purchase orders they placed earlier or expediting vendors to get materials to keep the factory running. But how much of your cost of goods sold goes to vendors? In industry the range is from 35 to 85 percent. The average is close to 60 percent. What should your purchasing people be doing with this much money going to suppliers? I know what I would want them to do.

How much of your management capacity is wasted by concentrating on shortages? We often talk about the capacity of direct labor and rarely discuss management capacity. But your management team, just as much as factory workers, has a capacity limitation. If a large part of this capacity is diverted to shortages and answering customer complaints, then the residual is all you have left for other managerial duties. In some plants the president is the chief expeditor. In one plant, I asked to see the general manager and was told he was on the factory floor helping to get out the end-of-the-month shipments. How's that for wasting managerial time?

One way of measuring the productivity loss in a business is by looking at the shipments for each day of the accounting month. In most plants not much is shipped out in the first couple of weeks. Then things do start to leave but at nowhere near the rate necessary to meet the monthly shipping target. However, in the last 4 days a huge amount is shipped out, and the monthly target is usually met. The banana curve of Figure 11-3 is commonplace in too many industries.

Overtime costs can be plotted on the same graph and the curve will be almost identical. What is overtime but paying more for something that could be produced on regular time if there were no shortages? And we all know that as overtime increases, efficiency decreases and quality deteriorates. And making poor quality is as bad as making obsolete inventory. It's a productivity loss no matter how efficiently you made it.

Some companies have experienced significant improvements in productivity when their inventories were better managed. Quotes of 30 percent or even 40 percent productivity gains have been made by some companies. Ask your assembly supervisors, "If you had all the parts you needed when you needed them, how much more product could you assemble and ship?" The answer invariably is 10 to 20 percent. And you know they're sandbagging. They will never tell you how much extra they really think they can make. I guarantee that if you have any of the symptoms described above, this is a more fruitful productivity area to attack than any other. The potential gains are enormous and you can achieve them relatively

Fig. 11-3 Banana curve of shipments.

quickly. But it means looking at inventory quite differently than you have in the past and seeing the damage it can cause. Only then will the solution start to become clear.

Interest Rates

The need to finance increased inventories obviously has a significant effect on interest rates. Businesses take out more loans at times of inventory building, causing capital to become scarcer and rates to climb. Capacity expansion, which also comes at the same time as inventory building, puts a double hit on the availability of money. I know that treasury borrowing, inflation, and the fluidity of money internationally are also significant factors influencing interest rates. But inventory and capacity changes compound the problem. And high interest rates mean sending more profits to the bank manager, who cries all the way to the bank.

In 1981 it was estimated that the profits of U.S. industry were 45 percent lower than they should have been with a more traditional rate of interest. And the high interest rates occurred at a time when industry could least afford these payments. We were on the downside of business activity but still had high inventories and significant debt to service.

Pricing

Prices firm up and increase when demand grows, and they decline or are discounted when demand softens. When our products are sought after we charge more, and vice versa. But what effect does this have on our economy?

The real question becomes, how elastic is the demand for our products? Let's take the case described earlier in which the steel industry cut prices for oil-field tubing. Would this increase the number of wells drilled and therefore increase total demand? And could oil-field tubing producers support any increased demand domestically or would it mean more imports would be brought in? Would price cutting simply slow down the destocking process, so 1983's sales would be sold at a discount in 1982? The decision to cut prices was arrived at after a thorough analysis exploring the trade-offs (I hope). But would it have been better financially for domestic producers to hold prices, force the destocking to occur quickly, and then go back to a reasonable balance of supply and demand, with prices at profitable levels? The prospect of low prices might have meant a delay in the return to profitability until late 1983, instead of sometime in 1982.

The specter of competition from foreign steel producers was probably one of the factors in the equation that led to price discounting. And there are several domestic companies competing in this market, so if one decided to discount they all had to follow suit. But who gained? Or were they all losers to the inventory changes that caused the problem in the first place?

Many companies, especially raw-material suppliers, go through this cycle. Inventory-amplified demand oscillations create pricing changes way out of proportion to real end-product demand. Profits fluctuate the same way, with good years and bad years, again for no good reason other than inventory swings.

Inflation, that ever-present ogre, is also increased by these effects. Prices go up when demand exceeds supply (inventory building is occurring) and rarely fall that much when the inventory level is corrected. I know that I said prices fall when demand softens, and that is very true of commodities such as food, steel, and aluminum. But other products, such as manufactured goods, do not follow the same discount road as aggressively. The resulting inflation has a devastating impact on our whole economic structure.

Social Problems

How many social problems can we blame on inventory changes? It's difficult to answer the question precisely because obviously many factors other than inventory create social problems. However, a number of them are accentuated by our misman-agement of inventories.

Unemployment is greatly affected by inventory swings. When destocking is under way, every industry cuts back either hours or workers. This also affects the service industry, almost all of which is tied to manufacturing in some way or another. There is no question that some services, for example, repair and maintenance activities, run countercyclically to the busi-ness cycle, but these are the exception. Most service businesses are directly tied to the presumed health of the economy. Travel and leisure, restaurants, and even the medical profession see slowdowns in activity during the so-called recessionary phases.

The rise in unemployment causes people to relocate to other parts of the country to get work, and this often breaks up families for long periods of time. Transfer payments for unemployment increase, ballooning federal and state deficits and causing more treasury borrowing; this stops the full extent of the interest-rate reduction that could and should occur.

Other government assistance programs are started to mini-mize the full impact of unemployment. Training programs are provided to help people qualify for whatever jobs are available. Relocation expenses are sometimes paid for in severe cases. Use of all other forms of transfer payments, such as food stamps, increases, which takes money from the remaining workers in the form of taxes or causes still more deficits in budgetary spending. And taking money from those who are working reduces their buying, aggravating the recession. Def-icits are a cause of high interest rates and inflation, which makes everything cost more and depresses real demand again.

Protectionism

It's funny that we can all agree on free trade as a basic principle of life but react to foreign competition when it hits our given industry with a call for tariffs or other forms of governmental protection. Now I oppose unfair competition from any source, whether it is domestic or foreign. But I also oppose the protection of industries that through their own mistakes or mismanagement are now suffering from strong foreign competition.

Key factors encouraging foreign participation in our economy are lead times and inventories. Many industries, for example, bearings, steel, castings, and semiconductors, traditionally react to slightly increased demands with longer lead times. Put yourself in a purchasing manager's shoes. The lead time quoted by a domestic supplier increases from 4 to 20 weeks. The purchasing agent is paid to supply the factory or distribution system with the right things at the right time. This can't be done when needs must be predicted 20 weeks into the future, so the agent looks for alternative vendors.

The problem is that all the industries mentioned operate nearly in unison, so all the domestic suppliers of the commodity the agent is seeking have long lead times. Where else is there to go but overseas? Quality and prices are usually comparable if not better, and lead times are often shorter. So in comes a foreign product to compete with our own, simply because of delivery times. But they were invited in, by our own domestic suppliers, who then become upset when the economy retrenches and the foreign products won't leave. The tragedy in this whole situation is that the cause of imports is largely related to inventory and not to real demand. But once the foreign businesses are here and won't leave, there is a real-demand change, downward, because their suppliers are also offshore. The number of jobs lost to this factor alone in the last 10 years is enormous. We can't afford this much longer at the current rate. But tariff barriers are *not* the solution. I hope that a fuller understanding of the problem will lead us to the correct solution.

The Whiplash Effect

I hope it's now clear what inventories do to the total economy. They are an amplifier of demand changes throughout the logistics chain. Wild swings in operating rates of industry occur to accommodate small real changes in end-user demand. Order flow rates from one link in the supply chain to another are related to business confidence, emotion, lead times, and inventory variables, and not to real demand.

Figure 11-4 diagrams the whiplash effect that we all experience. It is exactly what happened in the oil-field tubing case but also mirrors the situation of other commodities. In 1973 and 1974, orders for all kinds of steel had pushed lead times out to 50 weeks and more. The steel industry recognized the stupidity of taking orders this far out and started an allocation program based on their customers' usage in the previous year.

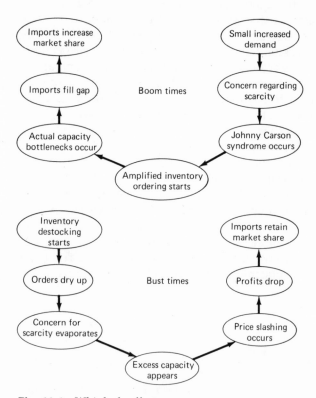

Fig. 11-4 Whiplash effect.

As soon as this started everyone believed there was a steel capacity shortage in this country, and maybe throughout the world. All steel customers took their full allocation and begged for more, even if they didn't need it.

Inventories of steel, at a time when there was a supposed capacity problem, increased dramatically. The steel makers were running their equipment as hard as possible, even taking the risk of bypassing regular maintenance activities. Overtime, additional workers, and other expenses were incurred to meet the orders. But a large portion of the orders represented fictitious demand, just inventory-building. Shortages of certain steel items placed even more pressure on the steel mills for even more production. When the crash came, as it had to, the steel industry went into a shock it hasn't recovered from yet. And you can see the impact on imports.

In any multilevel distribution chain, distributors, warehouses, factories, and vendors are all linked together. Decisions by any one of them to change inventories has a whiplash effect throughout the whole chain.

Even plants within the same corporation go through a similar cycle. Supplier plants and user plants are, in effect, in a chain. If decisions are made to change inventories anywhere in this chain, the whiplash effect takes over.

Inventories influence a huge part of our country's economy. They also affect other areas, such as the service industry. Our failure to manage and control inventories is causing untold disruptions, both social and economic. We must better understand the problems in order to solve them, and this means discarding some of our so-called common sense approaches. I hope you now have enough understanding of what must be done to make a contribution to the solution of these problems. For the future of an individual business or the total economy there are few problems more urgent.

Applicability to All Countries

This book has focused on America's industry and economy. Examples have come from American business papers and magazines to show that the theories presented in this book can explain what is really happening. I do not mean to slight other countries with this focus on the United States. It's simply because this is my home base, so I have more knowledge of conditions here.

The same effects *do* occur in other countries. Read *your* economic press, look at *your* country's economic performance indicators, and see how *your* company operates to prove it for yourself. This is a worldwide problem—with the possible exception of countries with controlled economies.

There's no point in talking about worldwide solutions or even national solutions. The inventory problem is just too big and unsuitable for such a grand approach. But we can attack the problem in small pieces. Each inventory management point, whether plant, distributor, or retailer, can amplify or dampen change. If enough people understand the problem and apply the right solutions, then we will have eliminated the major effects of inventory on the business cycle. And that is my hope.

Bibliography

Forrester, Jay W.: *Industrial Dynamics*, MIT Press, Boston, Mass., 1961.

Graham, Gordon: *Automated Inventory Management for the Distributor*, CBI Publishing Co., Boston, Mass., 1980.

Kersey, Bruce: "A Study Comparing Inventory-Sales Ratios with Various other Economic Data," *Production and Inventory Management*, first quarter, 1983.

Mather, Hal: "The Great Bathtub Mystery," *Inventories and Production*, vol. 2, no. 2, 1982.

Mather, Hal, and George W. Plossl: *The Lead-Time Syndrome Demonstrator*, George Plossl Educational Services, Atlanta, Ga., 1974.

Orlicky, Joseph: *Material Requirements Planning*, McGraw-Hill, New York, N.Y., 1975.

Plossl, George: *The Semiconductor Story—Did it Really Have to Happen?* G. W. Plossl & Co., Atlanta, Ga., 1976.

Plossl, George W., and W. Evert Welch: *The Role of Top Management in the Control of Inventory*, Reston Publishing Co., Reston, Va., 1979.

Shingo, Shigeo: *Study of Toyota Production System*, Japan Management Association, Tokyo, Japan, 1981.

Sirianni, N. C.: "Right Inventory Level: Top Down or Bottom Up," *Inventories and Production*, vol. 1, no. 2, 1981.

Stork, Ken: "A Successful Scheme for Managing Materials," *Inventories and Production*, vol. 2, no. 6, 1982.

Welch, W. Evert: "Controlling Inventory to Meet a Budget," *Inventories and Production*, vol. 1, no. 1, 1980.

Index